Kofi A. Annan
Prevention of Armed Conflict

Report of the Secretary-General

United Nations • New York, 2002

Published by the United Nations
Department of Public Information
New York 10017

United Nations publication
Sales No. E.02.I.13
ISBN 92-1-100891-3
Litho in United Nations, New York

Contents

Part One
Mandate and role of the principal organs of the United Nations

Part Two
Role of the United Nations system and other international actors

Executive Summary

Since assuming office, I have pledged to move the United Nations from a culture of reaction to a culture of prevention. In its presidential statement of 20 July 2000, the Security Council invited me to submit a report on the prevention of armed conflict, containing an analysis and recommendations on initiatives within the United Nations, taking into account previous experience and the views and considerations expressed by Member States. My first objective in the present report is to review the progress that has been achieved in developing the conflict prevention capacity of the United Nations, as called for by both the General Assembly and the Security Council. My second aim is to present specific recommendations on how the efforts of the United Nations system in this field could be further enhanced, with the cooperation and active involvement of Member States, who ultimately have the primary responsibility for conflict prevention.

In drafting the present report, I have endeavoured to take into account the many different views and considerations of Member States expressed in recent debates of the General Assembly and the Security Council on conflict prevention. It is axiomatic that the active support and cooperation of Member States will be needed for conflict prevention efforts to succeed. The specific contributions that can be made by the General Assembly, the Security Council, the Economic and Social Council, the International Court of Justice and the Secretary-General are explored in the present report, as is the cooperation between the United Nations and outside actors, such as regional organizations, NGOs, civil society and the business community.

The work of the United Nations system in the field of conflict prevention is not new. Many of the development and other programmes and projects of the United Nations system already have preventive effects or at least preventive potential, though they are often disparate and inchoate. My emphasis here is to show how the United Nations family of departments, programmes, offices and agencies (which have all contributed to the present report) interact in the furtherance of the prevention of armed conflict. Of particular importance are United Nations efforts for enhancing the capacity of Member States for conflict prevention. The challenge before us is how to mobilize the collective potential of the United Nations system with greater coherence and focus for conflict prevention, without necessarily requiring major new resources.

The basic premises of the present report are the following:

- Conflict prevention is one of the primary obligations of Member States set forth in the Charter of the United Nations, and United Nations efforts in conflict prevention must be in conformity with the purposes and principles of the Charter. Conflict prevention is also an activity best undertaken under Chapter VI of the Charter.
- The primary responsibility for conflict prevention rests with national Governments, with civil society playing an important role. The main role of the United Nations and the international community is

to support national efforts for conflict prevention and assist in building national capacity in this field.

- Preventive action should be initiated at the earliest possible stage of a conflict cycle in order to be most effective. One of the principal aims of preventive action should be to address the deep-rooted socio-economic, cultural, environmental, institutional and other structural causes that often underlie the immediate political symptoms of conflicts.

- An effective preventive strategy requires a comprehensive approach that encompasses both short-term and long-term political, diplomatic, humanitarian, human rights, developmental, institutional and other measures taken by the international community, in cooperation with national and regional actors.

- Conflict prevention and sustainable and equitable development are mutually reinforcing activities. An investment in national and international efforts for conflict prevention must be seen as a simultaneous investment in sustainable development since the latter can best take place in an environment of sustainable peace.

- A successful preventive strategy depends on the cooperation of many United Nations actors, including the Secretary-General, the Security Council, the General Assembly, the Economic and Social Council, the International Court of Justice and United Nations agencies, offices, funds and programmes, as well as the Bretton Woods institutions. The United Nations is not the only actor in prevention and may often not be the actor best suited to take the lead. Therefore, Member States, international, regional and subregional organizations, the private sector, non-governmental organizations, and other civil society actors also have very important roles to play in this field.

I am under no illusion that preventive strategies will be easy to implement. The costs of prevention have to be paid in the present, while its benefits lie in the distant future. The main lesson to be drawn from past United Nations experiences in this regard is that the earlier the root causes of a potential conflict are identified and effectively addressed, the more likely it is that the parties to a conflict will be ready to engage in a constructive dialogue, address the actual grievances that lie at the root of the potential conflict and refrain from the use of force to achieve their aims.

Governments that live up to their sovereign responsibility to resolve peacefully a situation that might deteriorate into a threat to international peace and security and call on the United Nations or other international actors for preventive assistance as early as needed, provide the best protection for their citizens against unwelcome outside interference. In this way, preventive action by the international community can contribute significantly to strengthening the national sovereignty of Member States.

In the present report, I have stressed that conflict prevention lies at the heart of the mandate of the United Nations in the maintenance of international peace and security, and that a general consensus is emerging among Member States that comprehensive and coherent conflict prevention strategies offer the greatest potential for promoting lasting peace and creating an enabling environment for sustainable development. The imperative for effective conflict prevention goes beyond creating a culture, establishing mechanisms or summoning political will. The United Nations also has a moral responsibility to ensure that genocides such as that perpetrated in Rwanda are prevented from ever happening again.

The time has come to translate the rhetoric of conflict prevention into concrete action. It is my earnest hope that the United Nations system and Member States will be able to work together in developing a practical road map to implement the specific recommendations contained in the present report. It is axiomatic that effective preventive action will require sustained political will and a long-term commitment of resources by Member States and the United Nations system as a whole if a genuine culture of prevention is to take root in the international community. The present report marks a beginning in that direction.

Kofi A. Annan
Secretary-General of the United Nations

1 Introduction

1.   Perhaps the most pitiful lesson of the past decade has been that the prevention of violent conflict is far better and more cost-effective than cure. The challenge is to apply that lesson so that prevention exists not just at the rhetorical level but also practically. This is easier said than done; existing problems usually take precedence over potential ones and, while the benefits of prevention lie in the future and are difficult to quantify, the costs must be paid in the present. On the other hand, the costs of *not* preventing violence are enormous. The human costs of war include not only the visible and immediate — death, injury, destruction, displacement — but also the distant and indirect repercussion for families, communities, local and national institutions and economies, and neighbouring countries. They are counted not only in damage inflicted but also in opportunities lost.

2.   The 1997 Carnegie Commission on Preventing Deadly Conflict found, for example, that the gross domestic product (GDP) in Lebanon in the early 1990s remained 50 per cent lower than it was before fighting broke out in 1974; that civil war and widespread use of landmines was widely blamed for the abandonment of an estimated 80 per cent of Angola's agricultural land; and that already inadequate food production in Burundi dropped 17 per cent during recent periods of conflict.[1] We also need to factor in the costs to external actors who intervene to stem the violence. A Carnegie Commission study estimated that the international community spent about $200 billion on the

---

[1]See *Preventing Deadly Conflict*, final report of the Carnegie Commission on Preventing Deadly Conflict.

seven major interventions of the 1990s, in Bosnia and Herzegovina, Somalia, Rwanda, Haiti, the Persian Gulf, Cambodia and El Salvador, exclusive of Kosovo and East Timor. The study calculated the cost differentials between these conflict management activities and potential preventive action, and concluded that a preventive approach would have saved the international community almost $130 billion.

3.   Nowhere are these lessons more glaring than in the Great Lakes region of Africa, where the failure of the international community to invest in prevention in Rwanda has had profoundly destablizing regional repercussions. Subsequent reviews by the United Nations, the Organization of African Unity (OAU) and national legislatures of some troop-contributing countries have agreed that there was ample early warning and opportunity for response to the "preventable genocide" of April 1994. Estimates by the Force Commander at the time, General Romeo Dallaire, that a deployment of approximately 5,000 troops to Rwanda in April 1994 would have been sufficient to halt the genocide have been borne out in subsequent investigations. The Carnegie Commission study estimated that the total cost of the augmented peace operation would have been $500 million annually and that preventive action in Rwanda would probably have cost $1.3 billion; in the end, the overall assistance to Rwanda in the wake of the genocide had a price tag of $4.5 billion.

4.   We have an obligation to the victims of violence in Rwanda and elsewhere to take seriously this challenge of prevention. I have pledged to move the United Nations from a culture of reaction to a culture of prevention. On 20 July 2000, the Security Council met to consider the role of the United Nations in the prevention of armed conflict. In a subsequent presidential statement, the Council invited me

to submit, by May 2001, a report containing an analysis and recommendations on initiatives within the United Nations, taking into account previous experience and the views and considerations expressed by Member States, on the prevention of armed conflict. As the nature of preventive action is such that, in its widest sense, it involves the whole United Nations system, I am hereby submitting the present report to both the Security Council and the General Assembly, which itself has adopted a number of resolutions relating to conflict prevention.

5.   My first objective in the present report is to review the progress that has been achieved in developing the conflict prevention capacity of the United Nations, as called for by both the General Assembly and the Security Council. My second aim is to present specific recommendations on how efforts of the United Nations system in this field could be further enhanced, with the cooperation and active involvement of Member States, who ultimately have the primary responsibility for conflict prevention.

Issues addressed by the report

6.   My basic premise is that the primary responsibility for conflict prevention rests with national Governments and other local actors. Without a sense of national ownership in each case, prevention is unlikely to succeed. Preventing the emergence of armed conflict requires early action by national actors and, where appropriate, by the international community. The earlier a dispute or inequity with the potential to lead to armed conflict can be identified and addressed successfully, the less likely it is that the situation will deteriorate into violence. Early action taken nationally to alleviate conditions that could lead to armed

conflict, with international assistance, as appropriate, can help to strengthen the sovereignty of States.

7.   For early prevention to be effective, the multi-dimensional root causes of conflict need to be identified and addressed. The proximate cause of conflict may be an outbreak of public disorder or a protest over a particular incident, but the root cause may be, for example, socio-economic inequities and inequalities, systematic ethnic discrimination, denial of human rights, disputes over political participation or long-standing grievances over land and other resource allocation. In many instances, the existence of such factors may lead groups to act violently in one society but not in another where appropriate and effective coping mechanisms exist, including well-functioning governance and rule of law institutions. The need for reliable early-warning information and a deep and careful understanding of local circumstances and traditions is therefore of great importance, and the fundamental inequities need to be identified and addressed in development planning and programming.

8.   The Carnegie Commission on Preventing Deadly Conflict described strategies for prevention as falling into two categories: **operational prevention**, which refers to measures applicable in the face of immediate crisis, and **structural prevention,** which consists of measures to ensure that crises do not arise in the first place or, if they do, that they do not recur. The present report will consider the broad spectrum of assistance offered to States by the United Nations system in the realm of both short-term operational prevention and long-term structural prevention.

9.   The Security Council has stressed the importance of responding to the root causes of conflict and the need to pursue long-term effective preventive strategies.

The Council has further noted that a coherent peace-building strategy, encompassing political, developmental, humanitarian and human rights programmes, can play a key role in conflict prevention. In this regard, I would like to draw a clear distinction between regular developmental and humanitarian assistance programmes, on the one hand, and those implemented as a preventive or peace-building response to problems that could lead to the outbreak or recurrence of violent conflict, on the other.

10.   An investment in long-term structural prevention is ultimately an investment in sustainable development: first, because it is obvious that sustainable development cannot take place in the midst of actual or potential conflict, and second, because armed conflict destroys the achievements of national development. In some cases, as we have recently witnessed, protracted conflicts have undermined the very existence of such States as Somalia and Afghanistan. Effective conflict prevention is a prerequisite for achieving and maintaining sustainable peace, which in turn is a pre-requisite for sustainable development. When sustainable development addresses the root causes of conflict, it plays an important role in preventing conflict and promoting peace.

11.   In the current era of diminishing international development assistance, the donor community is increasingly reluctant to provide development support to States that are on the brink of or in the midst of conflict. Investing in conflict prevention offers the potential for multiple returns for national development over the long term. More effective prevention strategies would save not only hundreds of thousands of lives but also billions of dollars. Funds currently spent on military action could instead be available for poverty reduction and equitable sustainable development, which would further reduce the risks of war

and disaster. Conflict prevention and sustainable development are mutually reinforcing.

12.   The role of the United Nations is principally to assist national Governments and their local counterparts in finding solutions to their problems by offering support for the development of national and regional capacities for early warning, conflict prevention and long-term peace-building. Such assistance is premised on the principle of consent of the affected Member States. In practice, international cooperation in this domain is often by invitation of the State or States concerned.

13.   The development and humanitarian agencies of the United Nations system, together with the Bretton Woods institutions, have a vital role to play in creating a peaceful environment, as well as addressing the root causes of conflicts at the early stages of prevention. The present report will examine how many of their regular assistance programmes can — and do — contribute to conflict prevention efforts, and how their effectiveness can be improved through greater coordination both of their efforts and with their respective host Governments. The report will also examine the tools that are available to the United Nations at later stages of prevention, which might include preventive diplomacy, preventive deployment of military and civil police contingents, preventive disarmament and allied measures, and effective post-conflict peace-building strategies.

14.   In drafting the present report, I have endeavoured to take into account the many different views and considerations of Member States expressed in recent debates of the General Assembly and the Security Council on conflict prevention. It is axiomatic that the active support and cooperation of Member States will be needed for conflict prevention efforts to succeed. The specific contributions that can

be made by the Security Council, the General Assembly and the other principal organs of the United Nations will be explored in the present report, as will the cooperation between the United Nations and outside actors, such as regional organizations, NGOs, civil society and the business community.

15.   The work of the United Nations system in the field of conflict prevention is not new. Many of the development and other programmes and projects of the United Nations system already have preventive effects or at least preventive potential, though they are often disparate and inchoate. Of particular importance are United Nations efforts to enhance the capacity of Member States for conflict prevention. The challenge before us is how to mobilize the collective potential of the United Nations system with greater coherence and focus for conflict prevention, without necessarily requiring major new resources.

16.   I take this opportunity to reiterate that a shift from a culture of reaction to a culture of prevention would be a major step forward. In the present report, I describe the practical actions that have been and are being taken to that end, based on United Nations mandates, experience gained and lessons learned, and I offer a number of conclusions and recommendations for the future.

Part One

Mandate and role of the principal organs of the United Nations

2 United Nations mandate for the prevention of armed conflict

A. The Charter framework

17. The cardinal mission of the United Nations remains "to save succeeding generations from the scourge of war". To that end, Member States have committed themselves "to take effective collective measures for the prevention and removal of threats to the peace ...", as set forth in Article 1, paragraph 1, of the Charter of the United Nations.

18. In my view, the Charter provides the United Nations with a strong mandate for preventing armed conflict. It also points to two defining elements of the philosophy underlying the collective security system: first, preventing armed conflict is a more desirable and cost-effective strategy to ensure lasting peace and security than trying to stop it or alleviate its symptoms; and second, armed international conflicts are best prevented by "peaceful means in such a manner that international peace and security are not endangered", as provided for in Article 2, paragraph 3, of the Charter. It is from this shared conviction with the drafters of the Charter that I have suggested that conflict prevention be made the cornerstone of the collective security system of the United Nations in the twenty-first century.

19. During much of the second half of the last century, collective security was largely pursued through reactive rather than preventive means, and was almost exclusively defined in military terms. That approach served some States well and remains valid. But, with the end of the cold war, a new understanding of the concept of peace and security has emerged. A broader focus on the nature of sustainable peace and its building-blocks, such as social and economic development, good governance and democratization, the rule of law and respect for human rights, is supplementing the traditional concept of collective security. In the twenty-first century, collective security should imply an obligation for all of us to strive to address tensions, grievances, inequality, injustice, intolerance and hostilities at the earliest stage possible, before peace and security are endangered. This, in my view, is the true core of a culture of prevention.

20.   This approach brings the United Nations back to its roots. Article 55 of the Charter explicitly recognizes that solutions to international economic, social, health and related problems, international, cultural and educational cooperation and universal respect for human rights are all essential for "the creation of conditions of stability and well-being which are necessary for peaceful and friendly relations among nations". The Charter thus provides the foundation for a comprehensive and long-term approach to conflict prevention based on an expanded concept of peace and security.

B.   General Assembly and Security Council decisions and the views of Member States on conflict prevention

21.   Since the late 1980s, the General Assembly and the Security Council have strengthened the mandate of the United Nations for conflict prevention established in the Charter. The General Assembly, most notably in its resolution 47/120 A, entitled "An Agenda for Peace: preventive diplomacy and related matters", reaffirmed the important

role of the Secretary-General in preventive diplomacy, and invited him to strengthen the capacity of the Secretariat for the collection of information and analysis and to set up an early warning mechanism. In its resolution 51/242, entitled "Supplement to an Agenda for Peace", the General Assembly further highlighted the importance of improving system-wide coordination of United Nations preventive measures.

22.   The Security Council held open debates on conflict prevention in November 1999 and July 2000. During those debates, a large number of Member States expressed their overall support for prevention, albeit with different priorities for action. Some stressed the need to focus on the socio-economic root causes of conflict and called for an increase in development assistance to prevent conflict. Others identified the promotion of human rights, good governance, the rule of law and democratization as the most important areas for preventive action. A number of countries emphasized that preventive action should mostly be limited to measures under Chapter VI of the Charter, but noted that enforcement action under Chapter VII must remain a legitimate means of last resort to prevent massive violations of fundamental human rights or other serious threats to the peace.

23.   The presidential statements adopted at those two meetings underlined that early warning, preventive diplomacy, preventive deployment, preventive disarmament and post-conflict peace-building are interdependent and complementary components of a comprehensive conflict prevention strategy. That comprehensive approach to conflict prevention was further expressed in the Security Council's recent open debate on peace-building in February 2001, during which a large number of speakers empha-

sized that a well-planned and coordinated peace-building strategy can play a significant role in conflict prevention.

24. Conflict prevention was also a prominent theme during the Millennium Summit of the United Nations, at which leaders from all parts of the world supported my call to move the international community from a culture of re-action to a culture of prevention. There was a broad con-sensus that the most promising approach was to develop long-term and integrated strategies, combining a wide range of political, economic, social and other measures aimed at reducing or eradicating the underlying causes of conflict. Both the United Nations Millennium Declaration adopted by the General Assembly in its resolution 55/2 and resolution 1318 (2000) adopted by the Security Council at the level of heads of State and Government recognized the vital role of all parts of the United Nations system in con-flict prevention and pledged to enhance the effectiveness of the United Nations in this field.

3 Role of principal organs of the United Nations in the prevention of armed conflict

A. Role of the General Assembly

25. Within the framework of Articles 10 and 11 of the Charter, the General Assembly has a broad authority to consider conflict prevention in all its aspects; develop recommendations, as appropriate; or call the attention of the Security Council to situations which are likely to endanger international peace and security. According to Article 14, the General Assembly may also recommend measures for the peaceful adjustment of any situation, regardless of origin, which it deems likely to impair the general welfare or friendly relations among nations.

26. I recall the useful work that the Assembly accomplished in this area by adopting resolutions 47/120 A and B, entitled "An Agenda for Peace: preventive diplomacy and related matters", particularly section VII of resolution 47/120 A, entitled "Role of the General Assembly in preventive diplomacy", and resolution 51/242, entitled "Supplement to An Agenda for Peace". Building on the precedents set in the past (e.g., South Tyrol in 1960; the Balkans in the Organization's first decade; and with regard to apartheid in South Africa), the General Assembly may wish to consider how it can make more frequent use of its powers under the Charter for the consideration of prevention issues in the future. To that end, the steps set out below could be considered.

Mechanisms for peaceful resolution of disputes

27.   The active use by Member States of methods of peaceful dispute settlements, as elaborated in Chapter VI of the Charter, is one of the most effective ways of preventing conflicts. The General Assembly has contributed over the years to the promotion of such practices, such as in its resolution 268(III)D 1949, on the establishment of a panel for inquiry and conciliation, and in its decision 44/415 on the resort to a commission of good offices, mediation or conciliation within the United Nations. The General Assembly may wish to consider making further recommendations on the use of such mechanisms within the international community.

Declarations, norms and programmes and creation of political will for prevention

28.   A more systematic attention by the General Assembly to conflict prevention would be instrumental in creating a truly global culture of conflict prevention through setting standards for accountability of Member States and contributing to the establishment of prevention practices at the local, national, regional and global levels. The Assembly has already worked actively in creating norms that have a bearing on the prevention of conflicts, such as in its resolution 43/51, which contains an annex entitled "Declaration on the Prevention and Removal of Disputes and Situations Which May Threaten International Peace and Security and the Role of the United Nations in this Field".

29.   In its resolution 53/243, the General Assembly adopted the Declaration and Programme of Action on a Culture of Peace, in which it called on Member States, civil

society and the whole United Nations system to promote activities related to conflict prevention. Within its wide area of responsibility, the General Assembly could also promote a culture of prevention in the multifaceted activities of the United Nations system. As in the case of its recent resolution on the Culture of Peace activities, the General Assembly could address the conflict prevention dimension of a number of items on its current agenda, such as disarmament, human rights, humanitarian assistance, democratization, environmental degradation, terrorism, acquired immunodeficiency syndrome (AIDS) and international law.

Deliberative functions

30.   General Assembly bodies, such as the United Nations Charter Committee, have already discussed issues related to conflict prevention and resolution. This kind of examination of new ideas and concepts by appropriate Assembly bodies should continue. The Assembly also receives reports from many United Nations bodies and agencies, which regularly include conflict prevention issues in their programmes. The United Nations University (UNU), the University for Peace and the United Nations Institute for Training and Research (UNITAR) submit their reports directly to the Assembly or through the Economic and Social Council and have programmes dealing with prevention issues. A discussion of these by the Assembly within a framework for elaborating a comprehensive prevention strategy would give them wider public attention and encourage more debate on prevention issues.

Interaction between the General Assembly and the Security Council on prevention

31. An important issue for the whole United Nations membership to consider is how to enhance the role of the General Assembly in conflict prevention as the Security Council strengthens its activities in this area. In the light of the Security Council debate that has emphasized the need to make peace-building part of a comprehensive conflict prevention strategy, preventive peace-building could be made a focus for a meaningful strategic interaction between the Council and the Assembly.

32. The Security Council deals mostly with potential conflict situations in countries which are not Council members. General Assembly members should have an opportunity for their views on conflict prevention issues to be heard more often in the Council. In order to bring about a more practical interaction between the Assembly and the Council, the President of the General Assembly and the President of the Security Council could discuss prevention issues in their monthly meetings. In order to assist the President of the Assembly to raise such prevention cases, the establishment of an open-ended group of Member States to assist the General Assembly President could also be considered.

Recommendation 1

I recommend that the General Assembly consider a more active use of its powers, in accordance with Articles 10, 11 and 14 of the Charter of the United Nations, in the prevention of armed conflicts.

Recommendation 2

I urge the General Assembly to consider ways of enhancing its interaction with the Security Council on conflict prevention, particularly in developing long-term conflict prevention and peace-building strategies.

B.   Role of the Security Council

33.   As the United Nations organ with the primary responsibility for the maintenance of international peace and security, the Security Council has a key role to play in the prevention of armed conflict. The basis for preventive action by the Security Council can be seen in Chapter VI of the Charter of the United Nations, which stresses the necessity to seek a solution to the continuance of a dispute or situation likely to endanger the maintenance of international peace and security. According to Chapter VI, the Security Council may investigate any dispute or any situation which might lead to international friction or give rise to a dispute.

34.   Although the Security Council has improved its transparency and working methods, its focus remains almost exclusively on crises and emergencies, normally becoming involved only when violence has already occurred on a large scale. I propose several means by which the Council could more easily identify and capitalize on windows of opportunity for preventive action.

Periodic reporting

35. In its presidential statements on conflict prevention of November 1999 and July 2000, the Security Council invited the Secretary-General to present periodic reports on disputes threatening international peace and security, including early warning and proposals for preventive measures.

36. I believe that periodic reporting is most useful when done as an informal and flexible practice rather than a scheduled obligation. It would also be more beneficial if such reporting could be set in a wider context. My meetings with the heads of regional organizations on prevention and peace-building, held in July 1998 and February 2001, respectively, showed that a comprehensive approach drawing on regional preventive strategies is a valuable one which should be pursued with our regional partners and appropriate United Nations organs and agencies.

37. I intend, therefore, among other approaches, to initiate a practice of providing periodic regional or subregional reports to the Security Council on threats to international peace and security. In most instances, such reports would relate to regional aspects of the issues already on the agenda of the Council and would thus complement current reporting obligations. The focus would be on cross-border issues that constitute potential threats to international peace and security, such as flows of illicit arms, natural resources, refugees, mercenaries, irregular forces and the security implications of their interaction. The reporting would also suggest priorities for action for the Council by identifying and reacting to such regional threats to international peace and security.

Security Council fact-finding missions

38.   In the past two years, there has been a welcome resumption in Council missions. While missions vary in their purpose and objective, they can have important preventive effects. After restarting the practice with one mission in 1999, there were five Council missions in the year 2000 — to Eritrea and Ethiopia, to the Democratic Republic of the Congo, to Sierra Leone, to East Timor and Indonesia, and for the implementation of Security Council resolution 1244 (1999) on Kosovo — as well as the recent missions in 2001 to the Democratic Republic of the Congo and other countries in the region and to Kosovo. The Security Council may also wish to consider using multidisciplinary expert support in its fact-finding missions to potential conflict areas so that all substantive areas can be incorporated into the elaboration of a comprehensive prevention strategy.

New mechanisms for discussing prevention

39.   As I proposed in my November 1999 statement to the Council, the Security Council could consider establishing an ad hoc informal working group, another subsidiary organ or other informal technical arrangement to discuss prevention cases on a more continuing basis. If established, early warning cases that I have proposed or cases suggested by the President or other Council members could be regularly referred to such a group before informal consultations or public meetings of the Council. When discussing cases on the agenda of the working group, its members could rely on the information received from individual members of the Council or information given by the Secretariat. The Security Council could also

consider using the Arria formula or other similar arrangements for informal discussions outside the Council chambers for exchanging views on prevention.

Recommendation 3

I encourage the Security Council to consider innovative mechanisms, such as establishing a subsidiary organ, an ad hoc informal working group or other informal technical arrangement to discuss prevention cases on a continuing basis, particularly with regard to periodic regional or subregional reports that I intend to submit to the Council, as well as other early warning or prevention cases brought to its attention by Members States.

C. Role of the Economic and Social Council

40. The Economic and Social Council has started to work more closely with the Security Council and General Assembly because the international community has recognized the value of an integrated approach to achieving peace, security, respect for human rights and sustainable development. A new phase began in 1998, when the Security Council invited the Council to contribute to designing a long-term programme of support for Haiti. Subsequently, it created the Ad Hoc Advisory Group on Haiti in 1999, which undertook an assessment mission to the country. The involvement of the Economic and Social Council was also requested in February 2000, when the Security Council proposed that it convene a meeting to discuss the impact of human immunodeficiency virus/acquired immunodeficiency syndrome (HIV/AIDS) on peace and security in Africa.

41.   More recently, in its resolution 55/217, the General Assembly requested the Economic and Social Council to consider the proposals of the Assembly's Open-ended Ad Hoc Working Group on the Causes of Conflict and the Promotion of Durable Peace and Sustainable Development in Africa, particularly on the creation of an ad hoc advisory group on countries emerging from conflict. An advisory group similar to that on Haiti has now been established for that purpose.

42.   I propose a more active involvement of the Economic and Social Council in the prevention of armed conflict, particularly because of its critical role in addressing the root causes of conflicts in the areas that lie at the core of its mandate. Its future contribution to the prevention of armed conflict and peace-building could take place either on its own initiative or as requested by other principal organs of the United Nations.

Long-term strategies to address the root causes of conflicts

43.   According to Article 62 of the Charter of the United Nations, the Economic and Social Council can initiate studies and reports in any area within its mandate. Such studies might be needed when it considers its specific involvement in the development of long-term strategies to address the root causes of conflict. The Economic and Social Council could use the various instruments at its disposal, including its subsidiary bodies, the Administrative Committee on Coordination (ACC) and its inter-agency machinery to draw upon the capacities of the whole United

Nations system to support the design and conduct of any such studies.

Regional perspective

44. The more active involvement of the Economic and Social Council could be beneficial when the Security Council sets up regional initiatives in the prevention of armed conflict. To that end, the Economic and Social Council should consider contributing to a comprehensive and multidisciplinary discussion on the prevention of armed conflict, particularly in a regional context. Since the Economic and Social Council is beginning to develop modalities to contribute to regional questions related to Africa in support of the work of the Security Council, the General Assembly and the Secretary-General in this area, that model could be extended to other regions.

High-level discussion on the root causes of conflicts

45. During the past years, the work of the Economic and Social Council has been greatly reinvigorated by the introduction of the high-level segment to its regular annual sessions. In the future, a high-level segment could be devoted to addressing the role of development, and the Economic and Social Council in particular, in preventing violence and conflict on a longer-term basis.

Recommendation 4

I suggest that a future high-level segment of the annual substantive session of the Economic and Social Council be devoted to the question of

addressing the root causes of conflict and the role of development in promoting long-term conflict prevention.

D. Role of the International Court of Justice

46.　The International Court of Justice, as an indispensable element of the system of peaceful settlement of disputes established by the Charter of the United Nations, has contributed over the years in a significant way to the solution of international disputes through peaceful means. The Court contributes to the peaceful settlement and resolution of disputes by delivering judgements in contentious proceedings between States. Conflict resolution is assisted when a dispute is submitted to the Court by special agreement or by an application by one State. Judicial proceedings can be suspended if the parties wish to pursue a negotiated solution. In addition, the Court contributes to the prevention of armed conflicts by facilitating the process of preventive diplomacy through rendering of advisory opinions on legal issues, an authority entrusted to the Court under Article 96 of the Charter. Through its judgements and advisory opinions, the Court has made a substantial contribution to the progressive development of international law and the identification of new trends that have been taking place in international law. The Secretary-General urges that States avail themselves of the Court to settle disputes.

47.　The International Court of Justice is more active today than ever in its history. Disputes from all corners of the world are brought before the Court. I urge Member States to make even greater use of the International Court of Justice in the future, inter alia, in the prevention of territorial and maritime disputes.

Compulsory jurisdiction of the Court

48. By the end of 2000, 60 Member States had made declarations accepting compulsory jurisdiction of the Court, albeit in many cases with reservations which tend to limit or narrow the effect of the compulsory jurisdiction clause. I would like to reiterate my appeal to Member States which have not yet done so to consider accepting the compulsory jurisdiction of the Court. I would also like to urge that States, when adopting multilateral treaties under United Nations auspices, adopt clauses providing for disputes to be referred to the Court. The more States that accept compulsory jurisdiction of the Court, the higher the chances that potential disputes can be expeditiously resolved through peaceful means. The Security Council should also consider recommending, pursuant to Article 36 of the Charter of the United Nations, that States submit disputes to the Court.

Advisory competence of the Court

49. In "An Agenda for Peace", (see A/47/277-S/24111), my predecessor recommended that the Secretary-General be authorized, pursuant to Article 96, paragraph 2, of the Charter of the United Nations, to take advantage of the advisory competence of the Court, and that other United Nations organs that already enjoy such authorization, turn to the Court more frequently for advisory opinions. However, the General Assembly did not act on these recommendations and the Security Council has not requested

any advisory opinion from the Court since 1993. Therefore, I urge both the Assembly and the Security Council to give renewed attention to the above recommendations, which I fully support, and to also consider authorizing other United Nations organs to request advisory opinions from the Court.

50.   I would also like to remind States of the availability of the Secretary-General's Trust Fund to Assist States in the Settlement of Disputes Through the International Court of Justice, pursuant to which financial assistance may be provided to States for expenses incurred in connection with disputes submitted to the Court by way of special agreement.

Recommendation 5

I urge Member States to resort to the International Court of Justice earlier and more often to settle their disputes in a peaceful manner and to promote the rule of law in international relations.

Recommendation 6

I urge Member States to accept the general jurisdiction of the Court. When domestic structures prevent this, States should agree bilaterally or multilaterally to a comprehensive list of matters they are willing to present to the Court.

Recommendation 7

I urge Member States, when adopting multilateral treaties under United Nations auspices, to adopt clauses providing for disputes to be referred to the Court.

Recommendation 8

**I recommend that the General Assembly author-
ize the Secretary-General and other United Nations
organs to take advantage of the advisory competence of the Court, and that other United Nations
organs that already enjoy such authorization resort to the Court more frequently for advisory
opinions.**

E.   Role of the Secretary-General

51.   The Secretary-General has had a role in the prevention of armed conflict since the earliest days of the Organization, through "quiet diplomacy" or "good offices of
the Secretary-General". The mandate for prevention is de-
rived from Article 99 of the Charter of the United Nations,
which provides that the Secretary-General may bring to the
attention of the Security Council any matter which in his
opinion may threaten the maintenance of international
peace and security.

52.   Preventive diplomacy is an important part of my
responsibilities, pursued through persuasion, confidence-
building and information-sharing to find solutions to difficult problems at a very early stage. I see the increasing demand for my engagement in this type of preventive action
as recognition that the Secretary-General can do much
quietly and discreetly outside the limelight of public attention,
even though the results may not always be visible or easily
assessed.

53.   There are three possible ways to enhance the
traditional preventive role of the Secretary-General: first,
by increasing the use of fact-finding and confidence-building
missions, as well as the appointment of high-level envoys

and the establishment of further regional liaison offices; second, by initiating joint preventive action by the Secretary-General and the Security Council; and third, by improving the capacity and resource base for preventive action in the Secretariat, which will be discussed later in the report.

Fact-finding missions

54.   The General Assembly and Security Council have encouraged the use of more fact-finding missions as part of preventive diplomacy. Fact-finding missions can provide an objective account of the interests of the parties to a potential conflict, with the goal of identifying the measures that the United Nations system and Member States might take to help reconcile or resolve their differences.

55.   Recently, I sent two inter-agency missions to West Africa. The first mission visited the Gambia in November 2000 for discussions with Government officials, political party leaders, representatives of civil society and members of the United Nations country team in order to explore with Gambian interlocutors possibilities for concrete United Nations assistance in addressing the country's multiple challenges with a view to preventing threats to peace and security in the country. The second mission, in March 2001, visited 11 countries in West Africa to take stock of the region's priority needs and challenges in the areas of peace and security, regional cooperation, humanitarian affairs and economic and social development, including the inter-linkages between them. I intend to use such interdisciplinary technical assessment missions more frequently in the future for preventive purposes, based on the full cooperation of the Member States concerned.

Confidence-building missions

56.   In "An Agenda for Peace", my predecessor indicated his desire to undertake periodic consultations on confidence-building measures with parties to potential, current or past disputes and with regional organizations, offering such advisory assistance as the Secretariat can provide. That approach was endorsed by the General Assembly in its resolution 47/120. In order to explore the scope for implementing that measure under the joint auspices of the United Nations and regional organizations, small missions could be sent to the capitals of regional States concerned, as well as to the headquarters of the principal regional organizations, to solicit their views on initiating cooperation at the working level on confidence-building in those regions.

57.   The dispatch of confidence-building missions could be a practical step towards the implementation of preventive diplomacy initiatives in a regional context, and to underscore the importance that I attach to the pre-emptive involvement of the United Nations in unstable regions. I intend to explore this option for preventive diplomacy in my future discussions with heads of regional organizations.

Informal network of eminent persons

58.   I intend to identify, after appropriate consultations, eminent persons to serve as an informal network for advice and action in support of my efforts to prevent and resolve armed conflicts. At times, members of the group might also be asked by me to engage in preventive diplomacy to contain or help to de-escalate emerging tensions.

Regional presence

59.   The establishment of the United Nations Liaison Office at OAU headquarters in Addis Ababa in 1998 constituted a first step in promoting cooperation, including on conflict prevention strategies, with regional or subregional organizations. I intend to explore the possibility of developing this concept, building on the precedent set in Addis Ababa.

60.   In October 2000, I established the Inter-Agency Task Force on West Africa, which is the first initiative by the United Nations to develop a coordinated and comprehensive approach to the prevention of conflict and to create the appropriate environment for peace-building in a particular subregion. The approach allowed for the examination of issues from both the national and subregional perspectives. The Task Force also sought to integrate the efforts of the United Nations with those of the Economic Community of West African States (ECOWAS), which collaborated in the conception and execution of the initiative and will be the major partner of the United Nations in the implementation of its recommendations. Among its recommendations is the establishment of a United Nations office in West Africa, to be headed by my special representative, that would enhance the Organization's capacity in the area of early warning, prevention, peace-building, reporting and policy development, as well as for collaboration with ECOWAS and other organizations in the subregion. Lessons from the West Africa initiative could provide a useful guide to United Nations conflict prevention efforts in other parts of the world.

Recommendation 9

With the support of Member States, I intend to enhance the traditional preventive role of the Secretary-General in four ways: first, by increasing the use of United Nations interdisciplinary fact-finding and confidence-building missions to volatile regions; second, by developing regional prevention strategies with our regional partners and appropriate United Nations organs and agencies; third, by establishing an informal network of eminent persons for conflict prevention; and fourth, by improving the capacity and resource base for preventive action in the Secretariat.

Part Two

Role of the United Nations system and other international actors

4 Role and activities of United Nations departments, agencies and programmes in the prevention of armed conflict

A. Overview

61.   Since assuming office, I have launched a number of initiatives to foster a culture of conflict prevention in the day-to-day work of the Secretariat as well as the wider United Nations system, based on the premise that sustainable development and long-term conflict prevention are mutually reinforcing objectives. Over the past five years, almost every part of the United Nations system, including the Bretton Woods institutions, has started to show an active interest in prevention and peace-building activities within the framework of their own respective mandates.

62.   Just as the root causes of armed conflict may vary widely, the nature of appropriate preventive actions and the resources needed to implement them cover a broad spectrum. The dimension of timing is also very significant: some preventive measures that may be practical if taken at an early stage may become inappropriate or even totally unacceptable as the dispute deepens and the outbreak of armed conflict grows more likely. Indeed, it could be argued that by the time the situation reaches the agenda of the Security Council it may be already a matter of late — rather than early — prevention.

63.   Conflict prevention can be addressed by a variety of approaches to achieve greater security and stability among States, including measures aimed at building mutual confidence, reducing threat-perceptions, eliminating

the risk of surprise attack, discouraging competitive arms accumulation and creating an enabling environment for arms limitation and reduction agreements as well as the reduction of military expenditures. Such confidence and security-building measures can be pursued at various levels, bilateral, subregional, regional and multilateral — even unilateral measures are conceivable — and can be applied flexibly to conform to the political and security characteristics and requirements of specific situations.

64. Looking at the United Nations system as a whole, the capability for preventive action is extensive. There remains, however, a clear need for introducing a more systematic conflict prevention perspective into the multifaceted programmes and activities of the United Nations system so that they can contribute to the prevention of conflict by design and not by default. This, in turn, requires greater coherence and coordination in the United Nations system, with a specific focus on conflict prevention. It also requires an enabling environment in which United Nations staff are encouraged to develop a proactive, preventive mindset, and in which incentives and accountability for preventive measures are put in place.

B. Measures to promote coherence within the United Nations system

65. Over the past several years, efforts to promote coherence within the United Nations system in general have increased. The ingrained habits of earlier years, whereby there was little exchange of information between departments and agencies, are increasingly being replaced by a readiness to share assessments and participate in joint efforts to identify and implement suitable and practicable

preventive actions. My emphasis here is to show how the United Nations family of departments, programmes, offices and agencies interact in the furtherance of the prevention of armed conflict.

Administrative Committee on Coordination

66.   ACC is the designated authority for promoting coherence within the United Nations system. The heads of 25 funds, programmes and specialized agencies, as well as the World Trade Organization (WTO) and the Bretton Woods institutions, participate under my chairmanship to promote coordination within the system. In 1997, ACC recognized the importance of reinforcing the system's overall capacity for early warning. It also agreed to the importance of peace-building as a broad-based approach to conflict prevention, and stressed the need to address the political, military, humanitarian, human rights, environmental, economic, social, cultural and demographic root causes of conflicts. In that light, I intend to engage ACC in a focused dialogue on what practical measures the United Nations system needs to take to promote greater coherence in its conflict prevention activities.

Executive Committees

67.   In 1997, as part of my programme for reform, I established a structure of four executive committees at the Under-Secretary-General level to act as internal decision-making mechanisms for the five main areas of concern: peace and security; economic and social affairs; development cooperation; humanitarian affairs; and human rights as a cross-cutting theme. Within this structure, the Executive

Committee on Peace and Security is well suited to deal with issues of system-wide preventive action. The Executive Committee on Humanitarian Affairs is the appropriate body to consider preventive and preparedness measures of a humanitarian nature, while preventive actions of a developmental nature are the natural purview of the United Nations Development Group (UNDG). The Executive Committee on Economic and Social Affairs gives upstream attention to root causes of conflict in terms of macroeconomic and social issues, governance and sustainable development. While most of their work to date has addressed issues other than conflict prevention, I intend to promote their more proactive use for that purpose in the future.

Interdepartmental Framework for Coordination

68.   Established in 1994 to strengthen planning and coordination among peacekeeping, humanitarian and political functions, the Interdepartmental Framework for Coordination has been reoriented towards early warning and preventive action since 1998. A Framework team, composed of senior representatives of 14 departments, agencies, programmes and offices, including the World Bank, meets monthly to exchange information from their respective areas of competence and to assess the potential for armed conflict, complex emergencies or other circumstances that may provide a prima facie case for United Nations involvement. The Framework has undergone constant development and improvement in accordance with General Assembly resolution 51/242, and is now becoming an important mechanism for early formulation of preventive strategies within the United Nations system.

Country-level coherence

69.   At the country level, the United Nations country team, led by the United Nations resident coordinator and in close cooperation with Governments, participates in an interdisciplinary process to develop the common country assessment, which has been completed in 70 countries, with another 40 in progress. The common country assessment analyses the national developmental situation and identifies key issues as a basis for advocacy and policy dialogue among the United Nations system and addresses national priorities and challenges, as well as regional concerns and initiatives. The common country assessment process leads directly to the United Nations Developmental Assistance Framework (UNDAF), which comprises the planning framework for developing programmes that encompass a coherent United Nations strategy for development assistance at the country level. The processes allow for key risk factors and prevention issues to be taken into consideration at an early stage in the programme cycle to promote common objectives and strategies of cooperation.

70.   Recognizing that one of the most serious threats to sustainable development is violent conflict, both the common country assessment and UNDAF offer a significant opportunity to identify and implement peace-building or conflict prevention strategies at the country level. The United Nations Development Group, therefore, should ensure that prevention and peace-building concerns are integrated into those processes, a critical step in laying the foundation for development programming that is carried out with a prevention lens, and that will enable United Nations country teams in partnership with national Governments and civil society, to address prevention concerns jointly at the country level.

71. The promotion of coherence for conflict prevention is also enhanced through the system-wide training programme for United Nations staff, entitled "Early warning and preventive measures: building United Nations capacity", which is conducted by the United Nations Staff College. This programme provides a forum for greater mutual exchange of views and coordination between United Nations agencies and offices dealing with both the policy and practical aspects of preventive action. These workshops complement the training being given to United Nations country teams on the common country assessment and UNDAF processes.

72. Coherence within the United Nations system needs to be complemented by a consistent approach of Member States in their policies towards the United Nations. Too often, departments, agencies and programmes have found that proposals, having received political endorsements from Member States in one forum, fail to win support from the same States in other — particularly financial — forums. When such disjunctures occur, institutional responsibility for activities can become blurred, complicating the efforts of the United Nations to develop effective approaches to conflict prevention. On the part of the Organization, to minimize miscommunication on this issue, I will work to ensure that the United Nations system makes as clear as possible a case for its resource needs.

Recommendation 10

I encourage the governing bodies and other intergovernmental bodies of the United Nations funds and programmes and specialized agencies to consider how they could best integrate a conflict prevention perspective into their different mandated activities.

C. Political action

73. Within the United Nations system, the Secretary-General's functions in the political area are supported by the Department of Political Affairs, which works closely with other departments, offices and United Nations agencies in many aspects of this work. One of the Department's key responsibilities is to follow political developments throughout the world and identify potential conflicts in which the United Nations could play a preventive role. It is also the focal point for prevention and peace-building in the United Nations system. To assist in this new role, the Policy Planning Unit in the Department was established three years ago. In 1998, it also established a new internal mechanism, the Conflict Prevention Team, which provides an intra-departmental forum for the development of preventive action options. In its capacity as Convener of the Executive Committee on Peace and Security, the Department also promotes discussion at the interdepartmental and inter-agency level and decisions on options for prevention.

74. The Department of Political Affairs has a mandate to identify potential or actual conflicts in whose resolution the United Nations could play a useful role. The four geographical divisions within DPA are each charged with identifying potential crisis areas and providing early warning to the Secretary-General on developments and situations affecting peace and security. To that end, desk officers of the four DPA geographical divisions develop country profiles on their respective countries and then monitor developments over time. By following what is the natural and normal course of political, social and economic life, they

are then well placed to detect changes and developments that may lead to crisis. With modern communications and online database services, there is a vast amount of information freely available to desk officers, but the Department still needs to develop further its capacity to use such information effectively and propose preventive action accordingly.

75.   If established, the new unit for United Nations–system-wide policy and analysis envisaged in the recent report of the Secretary-General on the implementation of the recommendations of the Special Committee on Peace-keeping Operations and of the Panel on United Nations Peace Operations (see A/55/977, paras. 301-307) could contribute to enhancing the Department's capacity in this field through its function as the secretariat of the Executive Committee on Peace and Security.

76.   Timely application of preventive diplomacy has been recognized by the General Assembly as the most desirable and efficient means for easing tensions before they result in conflict. To that end, the Department is endeavouring to develop more effective ways of undertaking preventive diplomacy. These include fact-finding missions, visits by special envoys to sensitive regions, the exercise of the Secretary-General's good offices and the establishment of groups of friends of the Secretary-General in different regions, composed of a few closely interested Member States.

77.   A considerable part of the preventive work of the Department of Political Affairs is done in support of special representatives and envoys of the Secretary-General, as well as field-based missions and offices. There are Department-supported missions currently in Afghanistan, Angola,

Papua New Guinea, Burundi, Guatemala, the Great Lakes Region, Lebanon, the Occupied Territories* and Somalia. Moreover, the Department of Political Affairs has established peace-building support offices in the Central African Republic, Guinea-Bissau, Liberia and Tajikistan. These offices work closely with government ministries, national assemblies, political parties, civil society and other local actors to support national peace-building efforts.

78.   The United Nations peace-building support offices can be instrumental, in supporting and closely collaborating with the country teams and non-resident United Nations agencies/offices, in developing multifaceted programmes that address many root causes of conflicts. Examples of this include improving support for democratic principles such as a fair role for the opposition, equitable access to public media, security sector reform, promoting tolerance and respect for human rights and providing technical assistance for the constitution and national institutions. In the future, the role of such offices could be extended, with the concurrence of Member States, to conflict-prone regions and countries.

79.   The work undertaken by the United Nations to support democracy in its Member States contributes significantly to conflict prevention. Such assistance encompasses the provision of comprehensive support in the area of governance and the rule of law, including electoral assistance. It has been proven to play an important role in preventing the breakdown of democratic institutions and processes, particularly in societies in transition, or in new or restored democracies. Since its establishment, the United

---

*Office of the United Nations Special Coordinator for the Middle East Peace Process and Personal Representative of the Secretary-General to the Palestine Liberation Organization and the Palestinian Authority.

Nations Electoral Assistance Division, for example, in co-operation with UNDP, has provided assistance in more than 150 electoral processes to enhance the administrative capacity of Member States to hold credible, transparent and fair elections, and to assist in the consolidation of democratic institutions. It is axiomatic that sustainable development can only be secured when people participate freely and effectively in decision-making processes.

80. The Department of Political Affairs is currently endeavouring to improve its early warning and analysis capacities; to improve the quality of its staff by training; to improve its coordination and cooperation with other departments, funds and agencies of the United Nations; to improve its cooperation with Governments and with regional organizations; to improve its outreach to research institutes and competent NGOs; to use the Trust Fund for Preventive Action to support the fact-finding and facilitation missions and other activities aimed at defusing potential conflicts and preventing existing disputes from escalating into conflicts. It is also strengthening its capacity to carry out its role as focal point for post-conflict peace-building in the United Nations system and to support the increasing number of United Nations peace-building operations, in partnership with other United Nations actors.

Recommendation 11

I urge the General Assembly to provide the Department of Political Affairs, in its capacity as focal point for conflict prevention, with adequate resources to carry out its responsibilities for conflict prevention and peace-building in the United Nations system.

D. Peacekeeping operations

81. While all peacekeeping operations could be said to have a preventive function in that they are intended to avert the outbreak or recurrence of conflict, their preventive role has been particularly clear where they have been deployed before the beginning of an armed internal or international conflict. This has taken place three times over the past decade, with the United Nations Preventive Deployment Force (UNPREDEP) in the former Yugoslav Republic of Macedonia, the United Nations Mission in the Central African Republic (MINURCA) and a succession of operations in Haiti. Apart from the shared feature that their host countries were not involved in a violent internal or international conflict, the common features included the possibility, or even the likelihood, of armed conflict, consent of the States concerned to the peacekeeping operations as the form of prevention, and the authorization of the operation by the Security Council.

82. The rarity of preventive deployment suggests that the international community has been reluctant to expend the political and financial capital required for a peace operation without the clear case for deployment that is made by open conflict. However, while success in a preventive mission is by definition hard to measure with precision, it is clear that there are circumstances in which preventive deployment of a peacekeeping operation can save lives and promote stability. The fact that conflict did not erupt within the host country during the above deployments strongly suggests that a United Nations preventive deployment operation, as a symbol of the international community's interest and as a source of leverage to promote its aims, may make a crucial contribution.

83.   Such experience shows that it may be necessary to maintain a preventive deployment for an extended period where the threats to security are ongoing, and that the achievements of these operations may need to be supported through longer-term follow-up peace-building action by the international community. In preventive deployment as in other forms of peacekeeping, a multi-dimensional approach will be required to address the root causes of conflict. The reform and restructuring of local law enforcement services; the disarmament, demobilization and reintegration of former combatants; mine awareness and mine clearance; and the development of human-rights and democratic institutions may all be essential parts of these efforts. It is also clear that, as with all peacekeeping, the ability of preventive deployment operations to contribute to lasting peace depends ultimately upon the readiness of the parties to take advantage of the opportunity before them.

84.   In the light of the close interrelationship between peacekeeping and peace-building, I welcome the recent presidential statement of the Security Council which reiterates the value of including, as appropriate, peace-building elements in the mandates of peacekeeping operations. In the light of the civil conflicts typical of the post-cold war world, particular emphasis needs to be given in this regard to civilian police, who have played an increasingly important preventive role in United Nations peacekeeping. Their contribution has been to restore public support to the local forces of law and order, whether by training the local police, monitoring their performance or assisting with the restructuring and reform of police institutions.

85.   In this context, some steps have already been taken by the international community to strengthen the foundations for civilian police engagement in peacekeeping. In 2000, the General Assembly provided some additional resources for support structures at Headquarters, while the Secretariat has sought to strengthen the policy framework for these efforts with the preparation of principles and guidelines for United Nations civilian police operations. However, further efforts are required in a number of areas which are the subject of detailed analysis in my current report on the implementation of the recommendations of the Special Committee on Peacekeeping Operations and the Panel on United Nations Peace Operations (A/55/977).

Recommendation 12

I encourage Member States and the Security Council to make more active use of preventive deployments before the onset of conflict, as appropriate.

Recommendation 13

I urge the Security Council to support peace-building components within peacekeeping operations, as relevant, and to strengthen Secretariat capacity in this regard, inter alia, through the measures outlined in my report on the implementation of the recommendations of the Special Committee on Peacekeeping Operations and of the Panel on United Nations Peace Operations (A/55/977).

E. Disarmament

86. The evolution of disarmament norms is a continuous process, and there are still some areas, such as missile development and small arms, which lack an international normative framework. Disarmament treaties and conventions contribute to the prevention of armed conflict through the promotion of the rule of international law. Wider accession to such multilateral treaties and their implementation with verification is essential for nations to feel confident that their security is assured.

87. Exchange of information and other forms of transparency in armaments and on military matters in general can help minimize the risk of misunderstanding or miscalculation, and can thereby contribute to greater trust and more stable relations among States. They can also serve as early warning mechanisms as well as encourage or lead to restraints in weapons acquisition by helping to identify the excessive or destabilizing accumulation of armaments. The Department for Disarmament Affairs operates and maintains two global transparency instruments: the United Nations Register of Conventional Arms and the United Nations standardized instrument for reporting military expenditures.

88. I have stated in my Millennium Report (A/54/2000) that small arms proliferation is not merely a security issue; it is also an issue of human rights and of development. The proliferation of small arms sustains and exacerbates armed conflicts, endangers peacekeepers and humanitarian workers, undermines respect for international humanitarian law, threatens legitimate but weak Governments, and benefits terrorists and the perpetrators of organized crime. Measures to prevent the misuse and illicit transfers of small arms and to address the root causes

of the demand for small arms would greatly contribute to the prevention of conflict.

89. Practical disarmament measures have gained wide recognition, particularly "weapons for development" projects aimed at the retrieval and collection of illegal weapons in exchange for community-based development incentives. In addition to the retrieval of illicit arms from the civilian population, as well as of weapons in possession of former combatants, the destruction and disposal of such stocks can help to prevent conflict or its recurrence by reducing the volume in circulation and the easy availability of such arms, which are often recycled from one conflict to another.

90. In the field of practical disarmament measures, the Department for Disarmament Affairs works with the Group of Interested States, which was established in March 1998 on the basis of a General Assembly resolution to promote practical disarmament measures, particularly to support peace-building efforts in post-conflict situations, while UNDP has worked since 1998 to design and support weapons collection, management and destruction projects through the UNDP Trust Fund on Small Arms. As a basis for these activities, fact-finding missions are undertaken by the Department, normally with the support of the Department of Political Affairs, UNDP and others, before project proposals are finalized. Field-level small arms assessments, which help to develop local and donor strategies and project level interventions, are also continuously carried out by UNDP within the development context.

91. The Department for Disarmament Affairs and UNDP are engaged in assisting Member States, upon their request, to address the problems posed by the proliferation of small arms and light weapons, particularly in the context of peace-building in post-conflict situations. In

June 1998, I established a mechanism, Coordinating Action on Small Arms (CASA), to harmonize all actions on small arms within the United Nations system, designating the Department as the focal point of the mechanism. CASA includes all departments and agencies with an interest in one or more aspects of the multidimensional threat posed by the proliferation of small arms and their misuse. The Department is also providing substantive support for the first United Nations Conference on Illicit Trade in Small Arms and Light Weapons in All Its Aspects to be held at United Nations Headquarters in July 2001, aimed at establishing a programme of action to curb the illicit trade in small arms and light weapons.

92.   The Department for Disarmament Affairs, together with UNDP, played a lead role in designing a "weapons for development" project, in cooperation with UNDP, for implementation in the district of Gramsch, Albania, following a request from the Albanian Government for assistance in retrieving small arms and light weapons illegally acquired by the civil population during disturbances in 1997. Similar projects have since been initiated in other districts of Albania. The concept of "weapons for development" has also attracted attention and interest in other regions. The de-weaponization of conflict-prone societies is therefore an important conflict prevention exercise.

93.   In addition to conflict-prone societies, the de-weaponization of post-conflict societies is equally important to prevent a relapse into conflict. It is important in this respect that the international community assist with adequate resources in disarmament, demobilization and reintegration efforts. The World Bank is playing an important role in this field, by providing technical assistance on the preparation of comprehensive disarmament, demobilization and reintegration programmes, assisting with the

reintegration of ex-combatants into civil society and advising on governance and public expenditure issues. Humanitarian partners also play a key role in disarmament, demobilization and reintegration exercises. For instance, since the early 1990s the World Food Programme (WFP) has been a primary partner in United Nations supported demobilization programmes (in Namibia, Angola, Mozambique, Liberia, Sierra Leone and Eritrea). Experience demonstrates the importance of an early involvement by humanitarian partners in the planning of demobilization and reintegration programmes, given the importance of humanitarian and rehabilitation assistance during the implementation of demobilization and reintegration programmes and their aftermath. Experience in Liberia and Sierra Leone offered a sobering example of how failure to provide adequate resources for disarmament, demobilization and reintegration efforts can contribute to the renewal of violence.

Recommendation 14

I encourage greater transparency by Member States on military matters, including broader participation in the United Nations instruments relating to arms transparency and military expenditure. I also call on the General Assembly and other United Nations disarmament bodies to strengthen existing disarmament-related early warning and transparency mechanisms, particularly with regard to small arms and light weapons.

Recommendation 15

In order to prevent the recurrence of conflict, I encourage the Security Council to include, as appropriate, a disarmament, demobilization and

reintegration component in the mandates of United Nations peacekeeping and peace-building operations.

F.   Human rights action

94.   Sustainable and long-term prevention of armed conflict must include a focus on strengthening respect for human rights and addressing core issues of human rights violations, wherever these occur. Efforts to prevent armed conflict should promote a broad range of human rights, including not only civil and political rights but also economic, social and cultural rights, including the right to development.

95.   In its resolution 48/141, the General Assembly requested the Office of the United Nations High Commissioner for Human Rights (OHCHR) to play an active role in preventing the continuation of human rights violations throughout the world. The report of the High Commissioner to the Commission on Human Rights at its fifty-sixth session (E/CN.4/2000/12) stressed the importance of strengthening preventive strategies in many different areas of human rights.

96.   In an effort to strengthen human rights protection capacities and thus contribute to conflict prevention, OHCHR is implementing over 50 technical cooperation projects, in collaboration with States, United Nations agencies and regional partners, to help Governments, national institutions and NGOs enhance their capacity in the area of human rights. These activities and education programmes strengthen the rule of law and build the human rights capacity of Member States. Information from human rights special procedures and treaty bodies, as well as information from OHCHR field presences, should be better integrated in the development of preventive strategies. Field offices of OHCHR also have a role to play in preventive processes.

97.   The International Criminal Court (ICC) will have a vital role to play in deterring the most flagrant violations of human rights through the enforcement of international criminal responsibility. Pending the establishment of the court, judicial bodies, such as the international tribunals for Rwanda and the former Yugoslavia, as well as jurisdiction established under human rights treaties, can also contribute to conflict prevention by enforcing individual accountability for such crimes and deterring future violations. Of particular importance in this regard are the ratification and implementation of human rights treaties by Member States and the ratification of or accession to the statute of the International Criminal Court.

98.   From 31 August to 7 September 2001, the World Conference Against Racism, Racial Discrimination, Xenophobia and Related Intolerance will discuss many of the issues linked to racial and ethnic conflicts, and I hope that it will make concrete recommendations, including on early warning systems, confidence-building measures and structural and institutional support mechanisms to prevent the deterioration of ethnic tensions into armed conflict.

Recommendation 16

I call on the Security Council and the General Assembly to make full use of information and analyses emanating from United Nations human rights mechanisms and bodies in its efforts to prevent armed conflicts.

Recommendation 17

I urge Member States to ratify or accede to human rights treaties and the statute of the International Criminal Court, if they have not already done so.

G. Developmental assistance

99. Development assistance cannot by itself prevent or end conflict. It can, however, facilitate the creation of opportunities and the political, economic and social spaces within which indigenous actors can identify, develop and use the resources necessary to build a peaceful, equitable and just society. Experience also shows that development will be sustainable only if development strategies incorporate concern for their impact on tensions that could lead to violence and promote measures to counteract such tensions. Wars and conflicts inflict loss of life and destruction, and put the affected countries further behind in their development, marginalizing them from the global economy.

100. Development assistance provided by the United Nations system needs to focus on decreasing the key structural risk factors that fuel violent conflict, such as inequity — by addressing disparities among identity groups; inequality — by addressing policies and practices that institutionalize discrimination; justice — by promoting the rule of law, effective and fair law enforcement and administration of justice, and, as appropriate, equitable representation in the institutions that serve the rule of law; and insecurity — by strengthening accountable and transparent governance and human security. In that light, there is value in United Nations resident coordinators exploring, where appropriate, and in cooperation with Governments, the setting up of a conflict prevention theme group mechanism at the country level to ensure the joint development and coherence of development strategies to address key risk factors.

101. In addition, United Nations development cooperation should aim to strengthen society's capacity for coping, managing and resolving tensions before violent conflict erupts. This includes providing assistance in strengthening governance in areas undergoing development that will help to address unstable situations, the judiciary, traditional conflict resolution mechanisms, the cultivation of political will and leadership for peaceful resolution of disputes, the development of conflict resolution skills and practices, consensus-building and public policy dialogue, and the promotion of participatory and inclusive decision-making on central economic, social and political issues. All development policies, programmes and projects need to be looked at through a conflict prevention lens so that socio-economic inequities and inequalities do not give rise to violent conflict. The conflict prevention lens approach needs to be incorporated into the common country assessment/UNDAF process.

102. At the request of Governments, the UNDP portfolio for governance and rule of law activities in countries prone to conflict now comprise more than half of UNDP programmes and activities, with an annual budget exceeding US$ 1.2 billion. In addition, a number of UNDP programmes support regional cooperation on cross-border issues (e.g., in the Tumen River Basin in East Asia) that have a clear conflict prevention impact. In post-conflict situations, UNDP area development programmes (e.g., Cambodia and Guatemala), small arms (e.g., Mali, El Salvador, Albania) and disarmament, demobilization and reintegration programmes (e.g., Mozambique, Guatemala) are aimed at preventing the reoccurrence of armed conflict.

103. A new generation of development projects is specifically focused on conflict prevention. For example, several UNDP-led projects in Romania, Bulgaria, the former Yugoslav Republic of Macedonia, Yugoslavia and Ukraine aim to create and strengthen early warning, conflict analysis and resolution capacities within government and civil society at the national and regional levels. The UNDP project entitled "Preventive development in the south of Kyrgyzstan" is another pilot project which seeks to enhance government capacities to undertake preventive measures as part of the process of nation-building, and identifies the importance of a regional approach to successfully effect preventive development. The Food and Agriculture Organization of the United Nations (FAO)-led Horn of Africa Task Force strongly recommends the creation of capacity in the region for early warning, conflict prevention and resolution, under the auspices of the Intergovernmental Authority on Development (IGAD) and OAU, as part of its Regional Food Security Programme. The UNDP project entitled "Capacity-building for the OAU mechanism for conflict prevention, management and resolution" is another example that addresses the issue from a regional perspective.

104. UNDP and the Department of Economic and Social Affairs are also collaborating with over 10 African conflict resolution institutions and practitioners to develop training material in four areas: conflict analysis and early response development, skills development for conflict transformation, conflict-sensitive approaches to development and national capacity-building in conflict management.

105. In recent years, there has been increased co-operation between the United Nations system and the Bretton Woods institutions, which have openly acknowledged that conflict seriously affects their development goals, and that understanding and working to prevent conflict should be considered a part of their mandates. This new approach has manifested itself in the establishment of a post-conflict unit in the World Bank and the new Operational Policy on Development Cooperation and Conflict adopted by the World Bank in January of this year. The World Bank's economic research on civil war is another area which has yielded important operational recommendations, which if implemented could reduce the risks of conflict.

106. As each organization increases its activities in post-conflict peace-building, which is an aspect of conflict prevention, the relationship has deepened. Examples of such cooperation can be found in East Timor and Haiti, among other places. However, contacts between the respective headquarters in this field have been limited and are only beginning to develop. Such contacts, especially at the working level, can assist both organizations in increasing their understanding of the situations they are both monitoring. Within their mandates and as appropriate, each organization should participate in the prevention structures of the other organizations. The World Bank's acceptance of the United Nations offer to participate in the Executive Committee on Peace and Security is a good example of this.

107. Contacts between the United Nations and the International Monetary Fund (IMF), which are at a more preliminary stage, need to be developed further. For example, the United Nations and IMF could work together to ensure that lending policies do not exacerbate social tensions and contribute to the eruption of violent conflicts. Several areas in which IMF plays a central role — particularly public spending — can affect the political situation in a positive or negative manner in the context of broader efforts for conflict prevention. In order to enhance coordination and interaction between the United Nations and the Bretton Woods institutions in conflict prevention and peace-building, the establishment of a consultative mechanism at the Headquarters level should be considered.

Recommendation 18

I urge Member States to avail themselves of the advisory services and technical assistance offered by UNDP and other United Nations development actors that aim to strengthen national capacities for addressing structural risk factors.

Recommendation 19

I call on donor countries to provide additional resources to strengthen the capacity of the United Nations Development Group to respond effectively to requests for assistance by Member States, to strengthen structural conflict prevention capacities and to facilitate South-South cooperation in this field.

H.   Humanitarian action

1.   General considerations

108.   While humanitarian action clearly plays a critical role in alleviating the plight of affected civilian populations in crises, humanitarian actors can also contribute to conflict prevention by implementing targeted projects to avert recurrence of conflicts. In countries and regions where there is a risk of persecution, violence and forced displacement, humanitarian agencies have a responsibility to develop an effective capacity for data collection and analysis so as to identify those countries that are at risk of being affected by humanitarian crises.

109. Preventing the internal displacement of civilians can play an important and at times pivotal role in the prevention of conflict. Unemployed and disaffected men and youth who are internally displaced, in particular those in internally displaced persons camps, are very vulnerable to recruitments (often forcible) by belligerents. By ensuring that civilians are able to remain at home and continue with their livelihoods and education, we can reduce the risk that they would become pawns in military action, thereby contributing to further conflict. Advocacy for the protection of civilians should be directed not only at the belligerents but also at members of the international community to take appropriate preventive action.

110. In ongoing humanitarian crises, advocacy and public information services conducted by the humanitarian community, along with consolidated appeals, are the primary examples of humanitarian action to raise awareness of a particular conflict and its consequences. Often, humanitarian activities create the only forum for divided groups to meet and to communicate — in itself a useful process for any future reconciliation. Humanitarian agencies have negotiated the creation of humanitarian spaces, routes or zones that have brought about a limited ceasefire to allow humanitarian assistance to reach vulnerable groups.

111. The support of Member States in the provision of protection to United Nations personnel working in insecure environments is of high importance. In this regard, the ratification of the 1994 Convention on the Safety of United Nations and Associated Personnel should be a matter of priority to all Member States that have not yet done so. It is also worth noting that humanitarian actors are often present in the field throughout the sequence of situations leading up to a crisis. This field-based presence gives them the unique benefit of first-hand information and analysis, which should be brought to the attention of the Security Council to take advantage of the opportunity for early preventive action.

Recommendation 20

I call on the Security Council to invite the Office of the United Nations Emergency Relief Coordinator to brief its members regularly on situations where there is a substantial risk of a humanitarian emergency. I also urge the Council to call for and support the implementation of preventive protection and assistance activities by United Nations agencies in situations where there is a risk of a humanitarian crisis. I request United Nations humanitarian agencies to integrate such preventive activities increasingly into their work in pre-crisis situations. In this regard, I call on Member States to provide increased resources for the work of these agencies in this field.

2. Specific aspects

112. The role of United Nations agencies and programmes in preventing conflict falls within their work in the four areas of food security, refugees, health and children, as described below.

(a) Food security and emergency food aid

113. Hunger and conflict are closely linked, in that in both internal and intra-state wars the control or disruption of food sources and supplies is often used as a means of waging war and/or as a means of starving out civilians from the opposing groups (e.g., Angola, Sudan, Mozambique, Sierra Leone). Food production and supplies are among the first casualties of a conflict situation. In addition, displacement prevents people from engaging in normal food production/acquisition activities.

114. When there is conflict there is an immediate increase in food insecurity, which makes the task of overcoming the root causes of conflict more difficult. Recent conflicts and farm invasions in southern African countries and the struggles between pastoralists and sedentary farmers in eastern Africa underline the importance of access to land-based resources by the poor as a basis for peace and sustainable development. Similarly, land concentration, coupled with poverty in Latin America, is one of the key issues underlying long-term conflict in that region. Where the need to meet family food requirements forces people to deplete natural resources or rely on degraded natural resources, WFP is seeking ways to provide food aid to support natural resource development activities and other land and resource management interventions. This can help prevent conflicts that are based on or related to tensions over limited natural resources.

115. Transboundary water supply could be a point of conflict or an opportunity for cooperation. There is evidence to suggest that good information on hydrology, among other things, has a role to play in the prevention of conflicts over water resources. FAO is currently assisting an extensive range of international basin organizations and regional organizations, such as the Southern African Development Community (SADC), in the formulation and implementation of joint water resource management strategies. Examples include the Nile Basin Initiative, the Lake Chad Basin Commission and the Niger Basin Authority. FAO also assists in the development of institutions for the management of common pool natural resources oriented towards reconciling conflicting interests in watersheds between upstream and downstream water users or in fish-producing areas between artisanal and commercial fishermen.

116. Although not always highlighted as direct objectives in WFP programming, preventive aspects are inherent in WFP work both in relief and development. WFP emergency programmes contribute to (*a*) (re-)establishing dialogue among (potentially) conflicting groups/parties; and (*b*) (re-)establishing a climate of confidence and trust among parties and towards the international humanitarian community. Road opening and transport infrastructure rehabilitation, at times accompanied by humanitarian mine action, may also have lasting positive effects by facilitating the free circulation of people and goods, the reopening of markets and contacts among separated communities across conflict lines.

117. By ensuring that its resources are targeted at vulnerable and marginalized groups and areas and by meeting their basic food needs, WFP can make an important contribution to social and political stability. Food aid can also be a catalyst for rehabilitation and development.

118. WFP and FAO are also important actors in the collection, analysis and dissemination of data and information concerning food insecurity and the related potential threats to vulnerable people and groups. The FAO *State of Food Insecurity* presents the numbers and proportions of the food insecure at the global and country levels. The Inter-Agency Working Group on Food Insecurity and Vulnerability Information and Mapping Systems seeks to improve the quality of information on the incidence, nature and causes of chronic food insecurity and vulnerability. The Global Information and Early Warning System assesses and reports the food supply situation and outlook (FAO) and the food relief needs (WFP) at the country level. The analysis of these indicators allows WFP and FAO to develop strategies that enable them to target the most vulnerable. Since 1999, WFP and FAO have been increasingly engaged in a process of sharing information with other partners, in particular through the United Nations Interdepartmental Framework for Coordination. An early warning function is normally in existence in all countries where WFP operates, often in association with Governments, United Nations agencies and other partners.

(b) Refugees

119. The interest and involvement of the Office of the United Nations High Commissioner for Refugees in prevention have been recognized in resolutions of the General Assembly, which has welcomed the commitment of the High Commissioner to explore and undertake activities aimed at preventing conditions that give rise to refugee outflows. The General Assembly has also called upon the High Commissioner to actively explore new options for preventive strategies that are consistent with protection principles.

120. Experience has demonstrated that the presence of UNHCR in zones of armed conflict has, in some situations, enabled the organization to intercede on behalf of people whose lives and liberty are at risk, to curb the worst excesses of the warring parties and to encourage other members of the international community to take appropriate political action. A vigorous public information, media relations and advocacy strategy, combined with more discrete diplomatic representations, can assist UNHCR in maximizing its preventative impact in such situations. In countries of asylum, the separation of armed elements from bona fide refugees and the effective maintenance of public order in refugee-populated areas also have an important role to play in preventing armed conflicts from arising and escalating.

121. It has become increasingly clear that the comparative advantage of UNHCR with regard to the prevention of refugee-producing situations is to be found in situations where armed conflicts have come to an end or diminished in intensity. Since the return of large numbers of refugees and internally displaced people to post-conflict situations can often act as a destabilizing factor, particularly when such returns take place rapidly, in large numbers and under duress, UNHCR efforts to consolidate the durable solution of repatriation by linking humanitarian assistance to longer-term development can greatly contribute to the averting of armed conflict. The potential for lasting political solutions will always be greater when returnees and others are able to become productive members of their own society.

(c) Health

122. The universal relevance of the issue of health care gives it salience as a means for preventive action. Health interventions, such as national immunization days, have opened avenues for dialogue and reconciliation, and their relevance should be considered not only in war-affected countries but also in conflict-prone zones. In Angola, the Democratic Republic of the Congo, Liberia, Sierra

Leone, Somalia, the Sudan, Afghanistan and Tajikistan, ceasefires and days of tranquility, negotiated between United Nations agencies and all parties in conflict, are key to polio eradication. For example, with the support of the United Nations Children's Fund (UNICEF) and the World Health Organization (WHO), in the Democratic Republic of the Congo, a breakthrough was achieved in 1999, when campaigns against polio vaccinated 8.2 million of the country's 10 million children under five. Following widely publicized appeals by the Secretary-General, fighting stopped in nine tenths of the country. Such immunization campaigns in United Nations negotiated days of tranquility can open windows of opportunity to dialogue between the different sides, and at critical moments can help to prevent the outbreak or escalation of armed conflict.

123. In sub-Saharan Africa, HIV/AIDS poses a particularly grave threat to economic, social and political stability. It threatens not only individual citizens but the institutions that define and defend the character of a society. There exists a potential risk for a rapid expansion of the HIV/AIDS epidemic throughout other parts of the world. During 2000, the General Assembly, the Security Council and the Economic and Social Council have all given this issue close attention. The forthcoming special session of the General Assembly on HIV/AIDS offers a particularly important opportunity to mobilize the international community towards more effective strategy for the prevention of HIV/AIDS and its potential destabilizing effects.

Recommendation 21

I urge the General Assembly at its forthcoming special session on HIV/AIDS to examine how strategies for the prevention of HIV/AIDS can be broadened to take into account the important

contribution that they can make to conflict prevention, particularly in seriously affected regions, such as sub-Saharan Africa.

(d) Children

124. Young people with limited education and few employment opportunities often provide fertile recruiting ground for parties to a conflict. Their lack of hope for the future can fuel disaffection with society and make them susceptible to the blandishments of those who advocate armed conflict. This problem can be especially acute in countries that have a "youth bulge", a population comprised of a large number of youth compared to other age groups. Such countries have often experienced higher amounts of political unrest, including violent conflict. Addressing the needs and aspirations of adolescence is therefore an important aspect of long-term prevention strategy. In addition, youth can also be an important resource for peace and conflict prevention, e.g., youth movements for peace and meetings of adolescents across perceived ethnic boundaries. UNICEF utilizes education in its programmes as a key strategy for preventing conflict and intolerance and securing conditions conducive to peace. Access by marginalized groups to education is another priority. Through programmes of education for peace, UNICEF seeks to foster a culture of peace, based on respect for human rights, tolerance, participation and solidarity.

125. Among factors that undermine a country's capacity to prevent disputes from turning into violent conflict are the scars left from previous bouts of violent conflict. The most poignant of these scars are those inflicted on children. The violence against — and witnessed by — children can incline entire generations towards the violent settlement of disputes. The cycles of violence generated by such abuses can also undermine whatever political will or leadership might exist for the peaceful settlement of disputes and steeply increase the cost to the international community of settling disputes.

126. My Special Representative for Children and Armed Conflict, UNHCR, UNICEF, OHCHR and many other intergovernmental and non-governmental organizations are working to alleviate the plight of children affected by armed conflict and to ensure their sustainable rehabilitation, which can contribute significantly towards a country's capacity for preventing the recurrence of violent conflict.

127. War-affected children should always be an explicit priority in efforts to prevent the initial occurrence of conflict as well as its recurrence, including in mechanisms to provide justice and reconciliation in the aftermath of conflicts. Through such means as the recently deployed child protection advisers, peacekeeping operations can also assist in the rehabilitation of children and thus in preventing the recurrence of conflict. The experience of UNICEF in the social and economic reintegration of demobilized child soldiers, such as in the Sudan, Sierra Leone and the Democratic Republic of the Congo, demonstrates that such activities are critical for preventing the recurrence of conflicts.

128. At its special session on children to be held in New York from 19 to 21 September 2001, the General Assembly will discuss issues related to children in situations of potential and actual armed conflict, and will outline appropriate strategies and actions for their protection.

Recommendation 22

I urge Member States to support policies and resources that target the needs of children and adolescents in situations of potential conflict, since this is an important aspect of long-term conflict prevention strategy.

I. Media and public information

129. Mass media has the power to shape and mobilize public opinion and is often manipulated by the conflicting parties to incite violence and to provoke armed conflicts. Control over mass media and the flow of information can be a decisive factor in shaping the outcome of a conflict. If the media is to be a restraining factor for the prevention of armed conflicts, an environment must exist that allows competing views to appear. Respect for the freedom of expression and the press is an important element of prevention.

130. The United Nations is often in a position to draw the attention of the international community to emerging conflicts through press statements, radio and television broadcasts, the Internet and public outreach activities, as long as this does not hinder efforts at quiet diplomacy. In particular, the direct and mission-based broadcasts of the United Nations, in concert with those of relevant international, regional and national broadcasters, can be used to counter hate messages in certain crisis situations and to reach target audiences in conflict-prone countries. There is also a need to promote "preventive journalism". Journalists and media organizations could be helpful in trying to identify specific situations before they erupt into armed conflict. United Nations departments and agencies should therefore incorporate public information into the prevention strategies being developed in their respective areas of competence. The public information activities of the United Nations should also incorporate preventive action into their programmes.

131. Most United Nations peacekeeping and political missions have some degree of public information capacity, and some of them have full-fledged information offices and media outlets to disseminate public information and respond to egregious media distortions and public misunderstanding of their operations. The presence of the United Nations may have a moderating role in the sense that it provides impartial information to the local population, and may help to reduce tension between the conflicting parties and prevent the resumption of armed conflicts.

Recommendation 23

I urge the General Assembly to provide additional resources for United Nations direct and mission-based broadcasts to counter hate messages and to promote media development in conflict-prone situations. I intend to reflect this priority in future budgetary submissions, as appropriate.

J. Gender equality

132. Ever since the First World Conference on Women, held in Mexico in 1975, there has been recognition that women have an important role to play in the promotion of peace. The Platform of Action adopted by the Fourth World Conference on Women, held in Beijing in 1995, and the agreed conclusions of the Commission on the Status of Women of 1998 further called on Governments and international organizations to protect women in armed conflict and support their participation in all aspects of peace support, including conflict prevention and post-conflict resolution and reconstruction. An essential aspect of conflict prevention is the strengthening of the rule of law, and within that the protection of women's human rights achieved through a focus on gender equality in constitutional, legislative, judicial and electoral reform.

133. In its resolution 1325 (2000), the Security Council recognized the differential impact of armed conflict on women and the need for effective institutional arrangements to guarantee their protection. The Council further recognized that the full participation of women in peace processes can contribute significantly to the maintenance and promotion of international peace and security. It also expressed its willingness to incorporate a gender perspective into peace operations, and called for measures that ensure the protection of and respect for human rights of women and girls, particularly as they relate to the constitution, the electoral system, the police and the judiciary. The resolution also called on me to expand the role of women in peace operations, to ensure that there be a gender component in field operations, and to provide Member States with training guidelines on the protection, rights and particular needs of women and on HIV/AIDS awareness in their national training programmes for military and civilian police.

134. The work programme of my Special Adviser on Gender Issues and Advancement of Women and of the Division for the Advancement of Women has contributed to findings and research in the area of women's role in peacemaking. The threats to all citizens, especially women, in conflict situations have underscored the need to incorporate gender analysis into early warning activities and the opportunity for preventive measures to strengthen women's protection. For a number of years, the Departments of Peacekeeping Operations and Political Affairs, UNICEF, UNHCR, UNDP and the United Nations Development Fund for Women (UNIFEM) have supported the incorporation of gender perspectives in peace support operations, through encouraging the participation of women in conflict prevention actions and providing assistance to women in conflict and post-conflict situations.

135. In order to ensure collaboration and coordination throughout the United Nations system in the implementation of Security Council resolution 1325 (2000), I have established a task force on women, peace and security. The task force, which is comprised of representatives from 15 United Nations entities, is in the process of developing an action plan on the implementation of the Security Council resolution. The action plan will outline initiatives to be taken by different parts of the United Nations system in relation to each of the operational paragraphs in the Security Council resolution. The invitation in the Security Council resolution to carry out a study on the impact of armed conflict on women and girls, the role of women in peace-building and the gender dimensions of peace processes and conflict resolution provides a particularly important opportunity for me to deepen the understanding of gender perspectives in conflict prevention and provide concrete recommendations for moving forward. In this context, Member States need to provide greater support to the efforts of the United Nations system to assist local women's peace initiatives and indigenous processes for conflict prevention, and to involve women in peace-building efforts, in accordance with Security Council resolution 1325 (2000).

Recommendation 24

I encourage the Security Council, in accordance with its resolution 1325 (2000), to give greater attention to gender perspectives in its conflict prevention and peace-building efforts.

K. Drug control and crime prevention

136. There is a need to address illegal business activities that fuel the fires of conflict. The United Nations needs to mobilize its considerable field presence in identifying and stemming the tide of illegal business activity. The activities of the Office of Drug Control and Crime Prevention could contribute to the prevention of armed conflict in two main areas: first, activities to counter transnational crime, particularly the illicit trafficking of drugs and money-laundering, diminish the fund-raising capacities of potential insurgents/aggressors; second, activities to curtail illicit trafficking in firearms reduce the availability of such weapons and thereby the readiness of antagonists to engage in armed conflict. In their work at the field level, United Nations country teams should give greater attention to the prevention of crime, drug trafficking and illicit trade in small arms. It is particularly important that as many Member States as possible should ratify the Convention Against Transnational Organized Crime and its Protocols, including the Protocol to Prevent, Suppress and Punish Trafficking in Persons, Especially Women and Children.

Recommendation 25

I call on the General Assembly, the Economic and Social Council and other relevant United Nations

bodies to provide increased resources for the activities of the Office of Drug Control and Crime Prevention, particularly in the prevention of transnational crime, drug trafficking and illicit trade in small arms.

5 Interaction between the United Nations and other international actors in the prevention of armed conflict

A. Regional arrangements

137. Regional organizations can contribute to conflict prevention in a number of specific ways. Such organizations build trust among States through the frequency of interaction, and have a greater grasp of the historical background of a conflict. Because of their proximity, regional organizations could, for example, provide a local forum for efforts to decrease tensions and promote and facilitate a comprehensive regional approach to cross-border issues.

138. Chapter VIII of the Charter of the United Nations provides a broad mandate for interaction between the United Nations and regional organizations in conflict prevention. To promote cooperation within this framework, since 1994 the United Nations and regional organizations have instituted a practice of holding biennial meetings.

139. In 1998, the Third High-level United Nations/Regional Organizations Meeting focused on the theme "Cooperation for conflict prevention". For the first time, we agreed on a framework for cooperation in conflict prevention based on 13 modalities. Over the past two years, meaningful progress has taken place with regard to coordination and consultation, better flows of information, visits of staff at the working level between the different headquarters, joint training of staff and joint experts meeting on specific cases for conflict prevention.

140. The Fourth High-level United Nations/Regional Organizations Meeting, held in February 2001, focused attention on the complementary theme "Cooperation for peace-building" in both a pre-conflict and a post-conflict environment. The Meeting adopted a document entitled "Framework for cooperation in peace-building" (S/2001/138, annex I), in which the United Nations and regional organizations agreed on guiding principles for cooperation in this field as well as on possible cooperative activities, such as establishing peace-building units, sending joint assessment missions to the field, developing repertories of best practices and lessons learned and the joint holding of pledging conferences. In its recent open debate on peace-building, the Security Council welcomed the results of the Meeting.

141. In recent years, a number of regional organizations have created innovative institutional capacities for early warning and conflict prevention. In 1993, OAU created the Mechanism for Conflict Prevention, Management and Resolution. In 1999, the Economic Community of West African States (ECOWAS) established a similar mechanism. The Organization of American States (OAS) designs long-term conflict prevention strategies through its Unit for the Promotion of Democracy, while the Policy Planning and Early Warning Unit of the European Union (EU) serves as its focal point for conflict prevention and peace-building. The EU is also in the process of developing a European programme for conflict prevention that will be considered by the European Council at Göteborg in June 2001. The Organization for Security and Cooperation in Europe (OSCE), through its Office of the High Commissioner on National Minorities and its Conflict Prevention Centre, also has an important capacity in the field. Other organizations are in the process of developing similar institutional capacities.

142. In addition, a number of cooperative arrangements ensure coordination and cooperation between the United Nations system and regional organizations and could be used for conflict prevention in a more targeted fashion in the future. The United Nations Office at Geneva, the Council of Europe, the EU and OSCE, for example, have established the practice of holding annual meetings to exchange views and coordinate efforts between them on matters related to their region. Another such example is the establishment of the United Nations liaison office at OAU headquarters in Addis Ababa in 1998.

Recommendation 26

I call on Member States to support the follow-up processes launched by the Third and Fourth High-level United Nations/Regional Organizations Meetings in the field of conflict prevention and peace-building, and to provide increased resources for the development of regional capacities in these fields.

B. Non-governmental organizations and civil society

143. Article 71 of the Charter of the United Nations recognizes the contributions that non-governmental organizations can provide to the goals of the United Nations. NGOs can contribute to the maintenance of peace and security by offering non-violent avenues for addressing the root causes of conflict at an early stage. Moreover, NGOs can be an important means of conducting track II diplomacy when Governments and international organizations are unable to do so. Such was the case in Mozambique and Burundi, where the Community of Sant'Egidio offered an impartial environment for divided groups to communicate and negotiate. International NGOs also provide studies of early warning and response opportunities, and can act as advocates in raising the international consciousness of particular situations and in helping to shape public opinion.

144. In recent years, academic and research institutes around the world, together with United Nations research arms, such as UNU, the University for Peace and UNITAR, have significantly increased their interest in early warning and prevention issues. I urge them to continue their endeavours and to bring their research results more effectively to the attention of United Nations practitioners and the political community. In this regard, United Nations field presences and field agencies in particular need to be more aware of the strengths and limitations of civil society actors in the area of conflict prevention and resolution.

145. A number of United Nations bodies have begun to develop programmes of collaboration with NGOs in the field of peace and security. UNIFEM, for example, has raised the profile of women by providing conflict resolution capacity-building to gender-based NGOs in the Sudan, Somalia and Burundi. Similarly, the Department for Disarmament Affairs maintains a broad relationship with NGOs in the field of small arms. NGOs were significant in the adoption of the Convention on the Prohibition of the Use, Stockpiling, Production and Transfer of Anti-Personnel Mines and on their Destruction in Ottawa in December 1997, and continue to play a major role in mobilizing local and international support for humanitarian mine action and for combating the proliferation and misuse of small arms.

146. An encouraging development during the past few years has been the growth of international and regional networks and directories of NGOs that deal with conflict prevention and resolution issues. In addition, an international networking capacity in the field of conflict prevention is currently being developed to systematically link academic experts, NGOs and other sectors of civil society to the United Nations and various other international and regional organizations. Another recently established initiative provides for online conferencing to facilitate exchange between scholars and practitioners for conflict prevention in a specific situation or region. It should also be noted that in May 2000, the NGO Millennium Forum urged the United Nations to involve a broad coalition of civil society organizations in more proactive conflict prevention efforts.

147. Religious organizations can play a role in preventing armed conflict because of the moral authority that they carry in many communities. In some cases, religious groups and leaders possess a culturally based comparative advantage in conflict prevention, and as such are most effective when they emphasize the common humanity of all parties to a conflict while refusing to identify with any single party. In addition, religious groups could mobilize non-violent alternative ways of expressing dissent prior to the outbreak of armed conflict.

Recommendation 27

I urge NGOs with an interest in conflict prevention to organize an international conference of local, national and international NGOs on their role in conflict prevention and future interaction with the United Nations in this field.

C. The private sector

148. The era of globalization has intensified the understanding that business is an integral part of the economic and political life of society. Along with this understanding, there is a growing recognition among international actors of the potentially important role that business can play in helping to avoid or overcome conflict.

149. I stress the need for transnational businesses to act with a social conscience in all their business activities. To that end, at the World Economic Forum in Davos in 1999, I launched the Global Compact initiative, a programme for establishing the business sector as a partner in peace by addressing the social consciousness of the international business community. The Compact calls upon business leaders to promote nine principles, both in their individual corporate practices and in supporting public policy in the field of human rights, labour and environment. Based on the assumption that societal stability and peace is good for business, in 2001 the Compact convened a series of dialogues on the role of business in zones of armed conflict in order to identify how businesses can strengthen human security within their sphere of influence.

150. It is also important that businesses should not contribute to economies that support conflict. In that context, I welcome the General Assembly's call on Member States in its resolution 55/56 to implement measures targeting the links between the trade in conflict diamonds and the supply to rebel movements of weapons, fuel or other prohibited material. Similarly, in its resolution 1343 (2001), the Security Council called upon all Member States to take appropriate measures to ensure that individuals and companies in their jurisdiction act in conformity with

United Nations embargoes. I also welcome recent Security Council resolutions that have established panels of experts to "name and shame" individuals and businesses that break sanctions or contribute to conflicts.

Recommendation 28

I encourage Member States and the private sector to support the Global Compact in the context of United Nations conflict prevention efforts. In particular, I encourage the business community to adopt socially responsible practices that foster a climate of peace in conflict prone societies, help prevent and mitigate crisis situations, and contribute to reconstruction and reconciliation.

6 Enhancing capacity for the prevention of armed conflict

151. Building and strengthening national capacity are essential in preventing armed conflict. In the present report, I have made a number of proposals for how the United Nations system could assist Member States in building such national capacity in more effective ways. The success of these recommended measures, if implemented, will depend to a large degree on whether they are backed by appropriate capacities and resources within the United Nations system as well as Member States. In that regard, I believe the areas described below need the attention of the international community for the strengthening of capacity in the field of conflict prevention.

Increase of official development assistance

152. Experience has demonstrated that equitable and sustainable development plays an important role in averting armed conflict. Although poverty by itself is not a root cause of violent conflict, the fact is that some of the poorest societies are either on the precipice or embroiled in armed conflict. Progress in the eradication of poverty and addressing, in particular, inequality, justice and human security issues in developing countries would greatly contribute to conflict prevention in the long term. For that reason, it is important that currently declining levels of official development assistance (ODA) be reversed as a matter of urgency. In that context, the recommendations of the High-level Panel on Financing for Development will have an important bearing on our future efforts in conflict prevention.

81

Enhancing capacity of Member States for conflict prevention

153. Arising from its successful staff training project, the United Nations Staff College is offering a new programme of country-specific workshops in conflict prevention for the benefit of Member States. The workshops aim to develop "home-grown" strategies for conflict prevention and to offer tools and techniques specifically designed to meet the needs of Member States. Participants include national government officials, members of civil society and representatives of United Nations country teams and their implementing partners. Other capacity-building activities of the United Nations system, such as UNDP activities aimed at strengthening governance and the rule of law, are also a good investment in developing national capacities, institutions and mechanisms for conflict prevention.

Enhancing the capacity of the United Nations system for conflict prevention

154. In the past two or three years, the United Nations system has made a promising start in engendering a culture of prevention in its day-to-day activities. Yet, within the Secretariat, an adequate capacity for conflict prevention is still lacking, despite calls for this in a number of General Assembly and Security Council resolutions and statements (see General Assembly resolution 47/120 A; Security Council resolution 1327 (2000); S/PRST/1999/34; S/PRST/2000/25; and S/PRST/2001/5), as well as in independent studies, such as the independent inquiry into the actions of the United Nations during the 1994 genocide in

Rwanda and the report of the Panel on United Nations Peace Operations (see S/1999/1257 and A/55/305-S/2000/809).

155. As demands for various peacekeeping, peace-making and back-stopping functions have increased in the Secretariat, the preventive function has clearly suffered. The Secretariat has no specialized staff in the regional divisions of the Department of Political Affairs or other units tasked to focus on conflict prevention activities on a full-time basis. As the culture of prevention gradually becomes more accepted, it is essential that the Secretariat be given an effective capacity for conflict prevention, including the capacity to systematically analyse successful and unsuccessful preventive efforts and apply them to the design of our future prevention strategies.

156. Similarly, the capacity of other relevant parts of the United Nations system for conflict prevention also needs to be strengthened. In that regard, the training course entitled "Early warning and preventive measures: building United Nations capacity" aims to improve the professional and analytical skills and awareness of United Nations staff and its implementing partners in the area of early warning and preventive action. Most of the courses have been held in the field, and United Nations participants have been drawn from 29 United Nations departments, programmes, offices, funds and agencies. Since 1999, some 750 United Nations Headquarters and field staff, participating non-governmental organization partners and nationals of Member States have benefited from this training. There is a need to expand this programme further in the future.

Inter-agency coordinating mechanisms

157. As discussed earlier in the present report, I have recently instituted inter-agency and interdepartmental co-ordination mechanisms in the field of conflict prevention that have started to show promise after an initial period of experimentation. Yet the Inter-Agency Framework for Co-ordination still suffers from a lack of effective follow-up and coordination due to resource constraints both at Headquarters and in the field.

Financial resources for Security Council missions

158. As noted in section 3.B above, the Security Council has recently made increasing use of missions to areas of tension or ongoing conflict. Yet the United Nations Secretariat has regularly encountered difficulties in securing financial and human resources in a timely fashion to support such missions.

Change of funding to the regular budget

159. While most of the recommendations contained in the present report will not require any new resources, there is a need for United Nations conflict prevention activities to be placed on a more stable and predictable financial basis. Although the generous contributions from Member States to the Trust Fund for Preventive Action are greatly appreciated, the General Assembly should consider whether activities related to preventive action should, as a rule, be funded from the regular budget rather than from extrabudgetary resources. In the coming months, I therefore intend to engage Member States in a dialogue on how conflict prevention could be made a regular component of the United Nations budget.

Recommendation 29

In the context of the long-term prevention efforts of the United Nations, I renew my appeal to the international donor community to increase the flow of development assistance to developing countries. I particularly urge Member States to give serious consideration to the recommendations of the High-level Panel on Financing for Development.

7 Conclusion

A. Overcoming the obstacles to conflict prevention

160. In the present report, I have stressed that conflict prevention lies at the heart of the mandate of the United Nations in the maintenance of international peace and security, and that a general consensus has emerged among Member States that comprehensive and coherent conflict prevention strategies offer the greatest potential for promoting lasting peace and creating an enabling environment for sustainable development. Moreover, it bears underlining that successful conflict prevention is also sound protection of development investment. I have demonstrated that both the principal United Nations organs and the United Nations system, through its broad range of departments, agencies, offices, funds and programmes, have increased their contribution to the prevention of armed conflict around the world.

161. The imperative for effective conflict prevention goes beyond creating a culture, establishing mechanisms or summoning political will. The United Nations also has a moral responsibility to ensure that vulnerable peoples are protected and that genocides never occur again. Yet, on two occasions in the recent past, in Rwanda and former Yugoslavia, the international community and the United Nations failed to live up to this responsibility. We have learned from those experiences that the very first step in preventing genocides is to address the conditions that permit them to occur. Two major reports that I commissioned on Rwanda and Srebrenica provide a compelling rationale for fully embracing a comprehensive programme of conflict prevention.

162. Yet we still fall far short. We are still far removed from a culture of conflict prevention in which States would seek the advice and assistance of the international community to help identify and address the root causes of conflict, whenever needed and at the earliest possible stage. Thus, the question remains: why is conflict prevention still so seldom practised, and why do we so often fail when there is a clear potential for a preventive strategy to succeed?

163. In my view, past experience offers two lessons in this regard. First, if the Government concerned refuses to admit that it has a problem that could lead to violent conflict and rejects offers for assistance, there is very little outside actors, including the United Nations, can do. To be successful, the United Nations must have the consent and support of the Government concerned and other key national actors for the implementation of a preventive strategy. Second, if important neighbours, regional allies or other Member States who would be well placed to support United Nations efforts lack the political will to lend their support, preventive action is again not likely to succeed.

164. It is clear that such attitudes alone are not the only obstacle to effective preventive action. No less significant are the ways in which the Member States of the United Nations define their national interest in any given crisis. Of course, the traditional pursuit of national interest is a permanent feature of international relations and of the life and work of the United Nations. But as the world has changed in profound ways since the end of the cold war, our conceptions of national interest have largely failed to follow suit. A new, more broadly defined, more widely conceived definition of national interest in the new century would induce States to find far greater unity in the pursuit of the fundamental goals of the Charter of the United Nations. A global era requires global engagement. Indeed, in an era of a growing number of challenges facing humanity, the collective interest *is* the national interest.

165. Of course there are constraints to a practical implementation of the collective interest. But what are the alternatives? The question is not simply one of academic interest. Most of the factors that stopped the United Nations intervening to prevent genocide in Rwanda remain present today. Yet if we do nothing — if we are quiescent in the face of war crimes and ethnic cleansing — we will not only risk being pushed to the margins of global politics but we will also betray the many millions who look to the United Nations for the implementation of the high ideals of the Charter.

166. Of course, as realists we must also recognize that in some cases the sheer intractability of conflicts and the obduracy of the warring parties will make our efforts unlikely to succeed. Moreover, in too many instances there are local warlords and other non-state actors who do not consider themselves constrained by decisions of the Security Council and the wishes of the international community. But even wars that cannot be stopped once started might have been avoided with effective preventive policies. I am under no illusion that preventive strategies will be easy to implement. The costs of prevention have to be paid in the present, while its benefits lie in the distant future. In addition, the benefits are often not tangible: when prevention succeeds, little happens that is visible, but the nurturing of societal stability, tolerance and sound institutions can be the foundations of sustainable peace.

167. The most promising approach for promoting the peaceful and just international order envisaged in the Charter is, as I have tried to demonstrate in the present re-

port, to build national and international capacity for long-term action to prevent armed conflict. The main lesson to be drawn from past United Nations experience in this regard is that the earlier the root causes of a potential conflict are identified and effectively addressed, the more likely it is that the parties to a conflict will be ready to engage in a constructive dialogue, address the actual grievances that lie at the root of the potential conflict and refrain from the use of force to achieve their aims.

168. Governments that live up to their sovereign responsibility to peacefully resolve a situation that might deteriorate into a threat to international peace and security and that call on the United Nations or other international actors for preventive assistance as early as needed provide the best protection for their citizens against unwelcome outside interference. In this way, preventive action by the international community can contribute significantly to strengthening the national sovereignty of Member States.

B. Towards a culture of conflict prevention

169. The present report provides ample testimony to the fact that the time has come to intensify our efforts to move from a culture of reaction to a culture of prevention. Based on the lessons learned and analysis presented in the present report, I propose the following 10 principles, which in my view should guide the future approach of the United Nations to conflict prevention:

 • Conflict prevention is one of the primary obligations of Member States set forth in the Charter of the United Nations, and United Nations efforts in conflict prevention must be in conformity with the purposes and principles of the Charter.

- Conflict prevention must have national ownership. The primary responsibility for conflict prevention rests with national Governments, with civil society playing an important role. The United Nations and the international community should support national efforts for conflict prevention and should assist in building national capacity in this field. Conflict prevention activities of the United Nations can therefore help to support the sovereignty of Member States.

- Conflict prevention is an activity best undertaken under Chapter VI of the Charter. In this regard, the means described in the Charter, for the peaceful settlement of disputes are an important instrument for conflict prevention, including such means as negotiation, enquiry, mediation, conciliation, arbitration, judicial settlement or other peaceful means, as set forth in Article 33 of the Charter. It must also be recognized that certain measures under Chapter VII of the Charter such as sanctions, can have an important deterrent effect.

- Preventive action should be initiated at the earliest possible stage of a conflict cycle in order to be most effective.

- The primary focus of preventive action should be in addressing the deep-rooted socio-economic, cultural, environmental, institutional, political and other structural causes that often underlie the immediate symptoms of conflicts.

- An effective preventive strategy requires a comprehensive approach that encompasses both short-term and long-term political, diplomatic, humanitarian, human rights, developmental, institutional and other measures taken by the international community, in cooperation with national and regional actors. It also requires a strong focus on gender equality and the situation of children.

- Conflict prevention and sustainable and equitable development are mutually reinforcing activities. An investment in national and international efforts for conflict prevention must be seen as a simultaneous investment in sustainable development since the latter can best take place in an environment of sustainable peace.

- The preceding suggests that there is a clear need for introducing a conflict prevention element into the United Nations system's multifaceted development programmes and activities so that they contribute to the prevention of conflict by design and not by default. This, in turn, requires greater coherence and coordination in the United Nations system, with a specific focus on conflict prevention.

- A successful preventive strategy depends upon the cooperation of many United Nations actors, including the Secretary-General, the Security Council, the General Assembly, the Economic and Social Council, the International Court of Justice and United Nations agencies, offices, funds and programmes, as well as the Bretton Woods institutions. However, the United Nations is not the only actor in prevention and may often not be the actor best suited to take the lead. Therefore, Member States, international, regional and subregional organizations, the private sector, non-governmental organizations, and other civil society actors also have very important roles to play in this field.

- Effective preventive action by the United Nations requires sustained political will on the part of Member States. First and foremost, this includes a readiness by the membership as a whole to provide the United Nations with the necessary political support and resources for undertaking effective preventive action in specific situations.

170. It is high time that we translate the promise of prevention into concrete action. Let us make this endeavour a testament to future generations that our generation had the political vision and will to transform our perception of a just international order from a vision of the absence of war to a vision of sustainable peace and development for all.

Security Council
Resolution 1366 (2001)

The Security Council,

Recalling its resolutions 1196 (1998) of 16 September 1998, 1197 (1998) of 18 September 1998, 1208 (1998) of 19 November 1998, 1209 (1998) of 19 November 1998; 1265 (1999) of 17 September 1999, 1296 (2000) of 19 April 2000, 1318 (2000) of 7 September 2000, 1325 (2000) of 31 October 2000 and 1327 (2000) of 13 November 2000,

Recalling also the statements of its President of 16 September 1998 (S/PRST/1998/28), 24 September 1998 (S/PRST/1998/29), 30 November 1998 (S/PRST/1998/35), 24 September 1999 (S/PRST/1999/28), 30 November 1999 (S/PRST/1999/34), 23 March 2000 (S/PRST/2000/10), 20 July 2000 (S/PRST/2000/25), 20 February 2001 (S/PRST/2001/5) and 22 March 2001 (S/PRST/2001/10),

Having considered the report of the Secretary-General on the Prevention of Armed Conflict (S/2001/574) and in particular the recommendations contained therein relating to the role of the Security Council,

Reiterating the purposes and principles enshrined in the Charter of the United Nations and *reaffirming* its commitment to the principles of the political independence, sovereign equality and territorial integrity of all States,

Mindful of the consequences of armed conflict on relations between and among States, the economic burden on the nations involved as well as on the international community, and above all, the humanitarian consequences of conflicts,

Bearing in mind its primary responsibility under the Charter of the United Nations for the maintenance of international peace and security and *reaffirming* its role in the prevention of armed conflicts,

Stressing the need for the maintenance of regional and international peace and stability and friendly relations among all States, and *underlining* the overriding political, humanitarian and moral imperatives as well as the economic advantages of preventing the outbreak and escalation of conflicts,

Emphasizing the importance of a comprehensive strategy comprising operational and structural measures for prevention of armed conflict; and recognizing the ten principles outlined by the Secretary-General in his report on prevention of armed conflicts,

Noting with satisfaction the increased recourse, with consent of receiving Member States, to Security Council missions to areas of conflict or potential conflict, which among others, can play an important role in the prevention of armed conflicts,

Reiterating that conflict prevention is one of the primary responsibilities of Member States,

Recognizing the essential role of the Secretary-General in the prevention of armed conflict and the importance of efforts to enhance his role in accordance with Article 99 of the Charter of the United Nations,

Recognizing the role of other relevant organs, offices, funds and programmes and the specialized agencies of the United Nations, and other international organizations including the World Trade Organization and the Bretton Woods institutions; as well as the role of non-governmental organizations, civil society actors and the private sector in the prevention of armed conflict,

Stressing the necessity of addressing the root-causes and regional dimensions of conflicts, *recalling* the recommendations contained in the report of the Secretary-General on Causes of Conflicts and the Promotion of Durable Peace and Sustainable Development in Africa of 13 April 1998 (S/1998/318) and *underlining* the mutually supportive relationship between conflict prevention and sustainable development,

Expressing serious concern over the threat to peace and security caused by the illicit trade in and the excessive and destabilizing accumulation of small arms and light weapons in areas of conflict and their potential to exacerbate and prolong armed conflicts,

Emphasizing the importance of adequate, predictable and properly targeted resources for conflict prevention and of consistent funding for long-term preventive activities,

Reiterating that early warning, preventive diplomacy, preventive deployment, practical disarmament measures and post-conflict peace-building are interdependent and complementary components of a comprehensive conflict prevention strategy,

Underlining the importance of raising awareness of and ensuring respect for international humanitarian law, *stressing* the fundamental responsibility of Member States to prevent and end impunity for genocide, crimes against humanity and war crimes, *recognizing* the role of the ad hoc tribunals for the former Yugoslavia and Rwanda in deterring the future occurrence of such crimes thereby helping to prevent armed conflict; and *stressing* the importance of international efforts in accordance with the Charter of the United Nations in this regard,

Reiterating the shared commitment to save people from the ravages of armed conflicts, *acknowledging* the lessons to be learned for all concerned from the failure of preventive efforts that preceded such tragedies as the genocide in Rwanda (S/1999/1257) and the massacre in Srebrenica (A/54/549), and *resolving* to take appropriate action within its competence, combined with the efforts of Member States, to prevent the recurrence of such tragedies,

1. *Expresses* its determination to pursue the objective of prevention of armed conflict as an integral part of its primary responsibility for the maintenance of international peace and security;

2. *Stresses* that the essential responsibility for conflict prevention rests with national Governments, and that the United Nations and the international community can play an important role in support of national efforts for conflict prevention and can assist in building national capacity in this field and *recognizes* the important supporting role of civil society;

3. *Calls upon* Member States as well as regional and subregional organizations and arrangements to support the development of a comprehensive conflict prevention strategy as proposed by the Secretary-General;

4. *Emphasizes* that for the success of a preventive strategy, the United Nations needs the consent and support of the Government concerned and, if possible the cooperation of other key national actors and underlines in this regard that the sustained political will of neighbouring States, regional allies or other Member States who would

be well placed to support United Nations efforts, is necessary;

5. *Expresses* its willingness to give prompt consideration to early warning or prevention cases brought to its attention by the Secretary-General and in this regard, *encourages* the Secretary-General to convey to the Security Council his assessment of potential threats to international peace and security with due regard to relevant regional and subregional dimensions, as appropriate, in accordance with Article 99 of the Charter of the United Nations;

6. *Undertakes* to keep situations of potential conflict under close review as part of a conflict prevention strategy and expresses its intention to consider cases of potential conflict brought to its attention by any Member State, or by a State not a Member of the United Nations or by the General Assembly or on the basis of information furnished by the Economic and Social Council;

7. *Expresses* its commitment to take early and effective action to prevent armed conflict and to that end to employ all appropriate means at its disposal including, with the consent of the receiving States, its missions to areas of potential conflict;

8. *Reiterates* its call to Member States to strengthen the capacity of the United Nations in the maintenance of international peace and security and in this regard urges them to provide the necessary human, material and financial resources for timely and preventive measures including early warning, preventive diplomacy, preventive deployment, practical disarmament measures and peace- building as appropriate in each case;

9. *Reaffirms* its role in the peaceful settlement of disputes and *reiterates* its call upon the Member States to settle their disputes by peaceful means as set forth in Chap-

ter VI of the Charter of the United Nations including by use of regional preventive mechanisms and more frequent resort to the International Court of Justice;

10. *Invites* the Secretary-General to refer to the Council information and analyses from within the United Nations system on cases of serious violations of international law, including international humanitarian law and human rights law and on potential conflict situations arising, inter alia, from ethnic, religious and territorial disputes, poverty and lack of development and expresses its determination to give serious consideration to such information and analyses regarding situations which it deems to represent a threat to international peace and security;

11. *Expresses* its intention to continue to invite the Office of the United Nations Emergency Relief Coordinator and other relevant United Nations agencies to brief its members on emergency situations which it deems to represent a threat to international peace and security and *supports* the implementation of protection and assistance activities by relevant United Nations agencies in accordance with their respective mandates;

12. *Expresses* its willingness to consider preventive deployment upon the recommendation of the Secretary-General and with the consent of the Member States concerned;

13. *Calls upon* all Member States to ensure timely and faithful implementation of the United Nations Programme of Action to Prevent, Combat and Eradicate the Illicit Trade in Small Arms and Light Weapons in All Its Aspects (A/CONF.192/15) adopted on 20 July 2001 and to take all necessary measures at national, regional and global levels to prevent and combat the illicit flow of small arms and light weapons in areas of conflict;

14. *Expresses* its willingness to make full use of information from the Secretary-General provided to him inter alia, under paragraph 33 section II of the Programme of Action in its efforts to prevent armed conflict;

15. *Stresses* the importance of the inclusion, as part of a conflict prevention strategy, of peace-building components including civilian police within peacekeeping operations on a case-by-case basis to facilitate a smooth transition to the post conflict peace-building phase and the ultimate conclusion of the mission;

16. *Decides* to consider inclusion as appropriate, of a disarmament, demobilization and reintegration component in the mandates of United Nations peacekeeping and peace-building operations with particular attention to the rehabilitation of child soldiers;

17. *Reiterates* its recognition of the role of women in conflict prevention and *requests* the Secretary-General to give greater attention to gender perspectives in the implementation of peacekeeping and peace-building mandates as well as in conflict prevention efforts;

18. *Supports* the enhancement of the role of the Secretary-General in conflict prevention including by increased use of United Nations interdisciplinary fact-finding and confidence-building missions to regions of tension, developing regional prevention strategies with regional partners and appropriate United Nations organs and agencies, and improving the capacity and resource base for preventive action in the Secretariat;

19. *Endorses* the call of the Secretary-General for support to the follow-up processes launched by the Third and Fourth High-level United Nations-Regional Organizations Meetings in the field of conflict prevention and

peace-building, and to provide increased resources for the development of regional capacities in these fields;

20.   *Calls* for the enhancement of the capacity for conflict prevention of regional organizations, in particular in Africa, by extending international assistance to, inter alia, the Organization of African Unity and its successor organization, through its Mechanism of Conflict Prevention, Management and Resolution, as well as to the Economic Community of West African States and its Mechanism for Prevention, Management and Resolution of Conflicts, Peacekeeping and Security;

21.   *Stresses* the need to create conditions for durable peace and sustainable development by addressing the root-causes of armed conflict and to this end, *calls upon* Member States and relevant bodies of the United Nations system to contribute to the effective implementation of the United Nations Declaration and Programme of Action for a Culture of Peace (A/53/243);

22.   *Looks forward to* further consideration of the report of the Secretary-General on Prevention of Armed Conflict by the General Assembly and the Economic and Social Council, as well as other actors including the Bretton Woods institutions and *supports* the development of a system-wide coordinated and mutually supportive approach to prevention of armed conflict;

23.   *Decides* to remain actively seized of the matter.

*Adopted by the Security Council at its
4360th meeting, on 30 August 2001*

Annex II

General Assembly Resolution 55/281

55/281. Prevention of armed conflict

The General Assembly,

Having received the report of the Secretary-General on prevention of armed conflict and the recommendations contained therein,[1]

Recalling its debate on the report on 12 and 13 July 2001,[2]

1. *Calls upon* Governments to consider the report of the Secretary-General and the recommendations contained therein;[1]

2. *Calls upon* regional and subregional organizations to consider the report and the recommendations therein addressed to them;

3. *Calls upon* all relevant organs, organizations and bodies of the United Nations system to consider, in accordance with their mandates, the recommendations addressed to them and to inform the General Assembly, preferably during its fifty-sixth session, of their views in this regard;

---

[1]A/55/985-S/2001/574 and Corr.1.

[2]See *Official Records of the General Assembly, Fifty-fifth Session, Plenary Meetings,* 106th to 108th meetings (A/55/PV.106–108), and corrigendum.

4.   *Invites* relevant civil society actors to consider the report and the recommendations therein addressed to them;

5.   *Decides* to continue to consider the report and the recommendations contained therein at its fifty-sixth session, taking into account, as appropriate, any views and comments received pursuant to paragraphs 1 to 4 above.

Adopted by the General Assembly at its
110th plenary meeting, on 1 August 2001

Index

Development assistance, 11, 22, 99–107, 152
Development investment, 160
Development policy, 101
Development strategy, 99
Disarmament, 29, 83, 86–93
Displacement of civilians, 108–109
Dispute settlements, 27–28, 46–50
Drug control, 136

E

Early warning, 7, 12, 21, 23, 39, 60, 71, 141, 156
Economic and Social Council, 40–45, 169
Economic Community of West African States (ECOWAS), 60, 141
Electoral assistance, 79
Environmental degradation, 29
European Union (EU)
  Policy Planning and Early Warning Unit, 141
Executive Committee on Peace and Security, 67
Executive Committee on Economic and Social Affairs, 67
Executive Committee on Humanitarian Affairs, 67

F

Fact-finding missions, 38, 53–55, 76
Food aid, 113–118
Food and Agriculture Organization (FAO), 115, 118
  Horn of Africa Task Force, 103
Food security, 113–118
Funding, 158–159

G

Gender equality, 132–135 *See also*: Women's advancement
General Assembly, 25–32, 169
  decision 44/415, 27
  resolution 268 (III)D, 27
  resolution 43/51, 28

resolution 47/120 A, 21, 26, 154
resolution 47/120 B, 26
resolution 48/141, 95
resolution 51/242, 21, 26
resolution 53/243, 29
resolution 55/2, 24
resolution 55/56, 150
Global Compact (Proposed), 149
Governance, 19, 22, 79, 100–101

H

Health, 122–123
High-level Meeting between the United Nations and Regional Organizations (3rd: 1998: New York), 139
High-level Meeting between the United Nations and Regional Organizations (4th: 2001: New York), 140
HIV/AIDS, 29, 40, 123, 133
Human rights, 19, 22, 29, 83, 94–98
Humanitarian assistance, 29, 108–128

I

Illicit trafficking of drugs, 136
Inter-Agency Task Force on West Africa, 60
Inter-Agency Working Group on Food Insecurity and Vulnerability Information and Mapping Systems, 118
Interdepartmental Framework for Coordination, 68, 157
Intergovernmental Authority on Development (IGAD), 103
International Bank for Reconstruction and Development (IBRD), *See*: World Bank
International Court of Justice (ICJ), 50, 169
  advisory opinion, 46, 49
  compulsory jurisdiction, 48
International Criminal Court, 97
International Monetary Fund (IMF), 107